YOUR INVINCIBLE POWER

*Open the Door to Unlimited
Wealth, Health and Joy*

PAMELA HAMILTON
and
W. T. HAMILTON

BALBOA.
PRESS

A DIVISION OF HAY HOUSE

Balboa Press books may be ordered through booksellers or by contacting:

Balboa Press
A Division of Hay House
1663 Liberty Drive
Bloomington, IN 47403
www.balboapress.com
1 (877) 407-4847

Because of the dynamic nature of the Internet, any web addresses or links contained in this book may have changed since publication and may no longer be valid. The views expressed in this work are solely those of the author and do not necessarily reflect the views of the publisher, and the publisher hereby disclaims any responsibility for them.

The author of this book does not dispense medical advice or prescribe the use of any technique as a form of treatment for physical, emotional, or medical problems without the advice of a physician, either directly or indirectly. The intent of the author is only to offer information of a general nature to help you in your quest for emotional and spiritual well-being. In the event you use any of the information in this book for yourself, which is your constitutional right, the author and the publisher assume no responsibility for your actions.

Any people depicted in stock imagery provided by Thinkstock are models, and such images are being used for illustrative purposes only. Certain stock imagery © Thinkstock.

Print information available on the last page.

ISBN: 978-1-4525-8996-1 (sc)
ISBN: 978-1-4525-8997-8 (e)

Balboa Press rev. date: 03/10/2017

When we think of Heaven we may relate to it as paradise, or bliss, or an abode of God, then again our portrayal may assimilate with a place of supreme happiness; a Shangri-La, or The Garden of Eden. Our thoughts venture to some sort of Utopia. I have come to know Heaven as something deep within our being, Our Soul. Our Spirit. It is the essence of love and happiness and all of the descriptions above and more. Love is Happiness. This ideal is the central nature of every human being living on the Earth. It is a vital element of our existence. All we need to do is reach deep within the core of our being and bring it to the surface. We have this ability to do so now, every single one of us. It is in the interest of our best well-being to bring this forth. This is what we have come to the Earth to do. If we succeed in our endeavors to do so, we can bring all of the love, all of the happiness and everything glorious into our lives now. We can reside in Heaven here on Earth. This is Our Invincible Power.

Pamela Hamilton.

Dedicated to the memory of my parents and sisters, Emily, George, Yvonne and Janice. I have been so fortunate to have had such a positive family. I know you are always with me in spirit.

Books by Pamela Hamilton and W.T. Hamilton

Your Invincible Power
How to Tame the Ego and Fuel Your Ambition

Your Invincible Power
How to Remove the Mental Hurdles and Limitations

Your Invincible Power
How to Say Goodbye to the Drama

Your Invincible Power
How to Create a Positive Relationship with Money

The Change 10
Insights into Self Empowerment

Love, Life and Beyond
(A Novel)

Contents

INTRODUCTION

"Our future is entirely within our own control. It is not at the mercy of any capricious or uncertain external power."
Charles Haanel (1866-1949) The Master Key System.

Think about this quote from *'The Master Key System.'* How different would your life be at this moment if you had complete power over it? What would you change in your life? What if you had all the money you needed, what would you do with it? What if you had wonderful relationships that are honest and loving towards you? How would you feel? What would your life be like if you had an abundance of health, physically and mentally and if you were full of energy? What if you were told that the quote above is absolutely scientifically correct and you do have complete control in all parts of your life? Wouldn't it be worth your while to look into it?

When W. T and I first discovered this new thought system we were in awe of it. We had discovered something unique and wanted to share it. We had been given an opportunity to change our lives and felt the need to pass this on, giving you the same opportunity we have discovered.

Through our own experiences and the astonishing events that have taken place since we have discovered this new way of thinking, we have designed an easy and reliable way to not only change your views, but to change your life in a magnificent way. These events have been a testament to us of the truth which we present within these pages.

In a fun way W. T. will bring to you important strategies and scenarios with easy to follow methods. He will take you through his own growth to success. I will facilitate my own observations of the masterworks of the great ones, and also of the teachers of today who pass these truths on, with guidance for our benefit. We only ask that you can open your mind, eyes and heart to these procedures which, we promise, will assist you and will transform your life the way it has ours.

Charles F. Haanel was a great business man, a leader, philosopher and visionary of his time. People of today have called him the *'Father of Personal Development.'* Well known for his classic, *'The Master Key System,'* published a hundred years ago. *'The Master Key System'* is one of the finest studies in self improvement and higher consciousness, and is still as popular today as it was one hundred years ago. This master works helped W.T. and I to change our way of thinking and therefore our lives. We have brought to you many of his ideas also, ideas that have made many millionaires and billionaires who they are today.

If you follow these ideas we are presenting to you, our hope is that you will be guided, as we are, to many truths, gain valuable insight into the way this natural law works, and learn how you can succeed in acquiring abundance in every way. Do you want to be rich? I believe we all do. From the words of the great ones we hope to shed a light on the questions we are all asking, the main one being, 'Why am I here?'

Eighty-five percent of Earth's entire population live in negativity from not only where we stand at this moment but to the far reaches of the Earth. And so our negativity draws us away from the good life we were meant to live. To substitute our negative thoughts for positive thinking takes some effort, however, you will see great changes start to appear in your life from the moment you begin to substitute this negative thinking you have constantly lived with up until now. We know, we have come from that place and we have seen and are seeing major changes in our own lives and in our environment daily in the most awesome ways.

Changing our views to the positive eventually transforms our energy fields from conflicting to unequivocal gratification, from poverty to riches, from disease to health, from loneliness to happy relationships. All of this is factual and has been proven to an exact science.

We live in the negative because we have never been acquainted with another way of thinking. We cannot be in control of our lives if we don't understand the powers we possess. Since we haven't been introduced to this way of thinking we let negative thoughts rule us. When we take this positive pathway, we begin to learn and understand about our deeper self from lessons that come our way. A door is opened and things become clearer to us. We see the hurt and pain that we contribute to ourselves daily and we begin to heal.

To put a spotlight on this hidden virus of negativity we have to delve into our own consciousness, and our beliefs, by taking control of our thoughts.

This starts with the understanding that we have a higher power which is with us throughout our lives and is waiting to help us reach special creative goals we have been given. We are all on a journey and when we understand our own power, life will support us perfectly in our quest. We are all a work in progress and we all deserve to be rich in every part of our lives. It is our right to be rich and abundant.

We are all in the process of evolving. We cannot *'not'* evolve. Gradually our collective psyche is seeing a new way of thinking and we will eventually collaborate at a higher energy rate—it is happening at this very moment, we are moving forward. Our spiritual teachers tell us about these exciting times, therefore, we come to understand that the entire human experience is changing and beckons to us to change with it. We are beginning to feel this attraction of change. It is drawing us ever closer. There is a great future cloaked in wonderful experiences, creativity and transformation, awaiting each of us if we claim it, which urge us on.

Our desire is to help you to become aware of these gifts, to evolve to a new you, to accomplish great goals by assisting you with new concepts, methods, and procedures to make the changes you desire.

Our hope is to deliver concrete material which will help you turn your life in the direction which you desire. The life that you deserve, a life full of abundance, health wealth, happiness and love weaved in fun.

Your friends,

Pamela Hamilton and W. T. Hamilton.

ONE

The Miracle of Us

*"We are sending our thoughts of greater or less intensity all
of the time, and we are reaping the results of such thoughts.
Not only do our thought-waves influence ourselves and
others, but they have a drawing power-they attract to us the
thoughts of others, things, circumstances, people, in accord
with the character of the thought uppermost in our minds."
William Walker Atkinson (1862-1932) Thought Vibration.*

Energy

Every human on earth is made of energy. We are made up
of cells, which are made up from atoms, which are made up
of subatomic particles. Which is Energy! This means our
thoughts too, are energy. They are not a static substance
which stays dormant and dissipates in the air as we have
always imagined. They are potent because the energy they
retain is the most powerful energy in the Universe, and
this energy is within our control since our thoughts are
completely under our control.

Only you can govern your thoughts. No one else can make choices in your life but you.

People can try and will influence you but only you can think what you want to think, therefore, take action upon the conclusion of those thoughts.

Thoughts are powerful energy that can bring us to the invincible life we've only dreamed of until this point in our existence. But before we can possibly use this power to our advantage we first have to understand it, we have to learn and allow this knowledge to penetrate. If we fail to come to an understanding of this knowledge, then we are missing the greatest gift that has ever come our way. It is like a person being given a beautiful new car, completely loaded with all the latest gadgets. It sits there shiny and powerful, they have the keys in their hand but they have never learned to drive. If they don't take the time to learn how to drive, the car will sit there. It will not bring them real joy without the driving lessons.

This new way of thinking changes our lives but we have to understand the dynamics which make us what we are and understand the choices we need to make. Quantum Physics and Spiritual Science have made amazing discoveries about this energy. Information gathered brought with it great progress, the results being, we are much more than static mind with a transient soul fleeting through this life like a fugitive for no particular reason. The question is: Are we born only to advance to what we perceive as death?

What would be the reason for our lives if this were the only answer? This powerful discovery unveiled a truth. This truth tells us the ultimate reason as to why we have come to this Earth. The conclusion being: Mind does not die but has always been, and can never 'not' be. The great men that have studied this concluded, every human being on this earth came with gifts of creativity, and it is these gifts each of us are searching for.

This is an unusual concept for many of us to contemplate but consider this; if mind lives forever then we have also lived other lifetimes, therefore, we have collected and now carry with us an identity made up of many different parts. This then is our personality. Some of these parts of ourselves may be vulnerable and weak or strong and overpowering. Some may be angry and yet some might be tranquil. We are all different, and yet we are all the same in the fact that we all have parts of us we need to heal.

That is why we are here. So there are many reasons for our existence and much knowledge for all of us to channel into. This is the mission each and every one of us are on.

Mind is said to be a subtle form of static energy, thought is active energy which is Omnipotent, Omniscient and Omnipresent, (not limited, knowing all things, always present.)

With this belief in view our Earth's population are on the same mission, there is no, 'We and Them,' we are all part of the whole, the only difference is one of degree. We all can tap into Omnipotent, Omniscient and Omnipresent energy, it is our right to. This includes all cultures, all people—no exceptions.

Only cultures, beliefs, and what we call inherited thoughts separate us. But with close examination of this, if mind lives forever, doesn't this tell us there is a great possibility we may have revisited this earth and have done many times prior to our life now? This leads us to the conclusion, anyone of us could be born in the other man, or woman's skin, living in their ways and under their belief system.

False beliefs reign in our mind unfaltering. False premises from others who have left us to feel powerless in many ways. We believe far more in the words of others and their truths. The truth is that it is imperative we change this way of thinking to be, do or have all what we desire in life.

To confirm some of the origins of this data that has been discussed I put forward some of the original findings to acquaint you with these powerful facts: Physics and Science have resolved matter into an immense number of molecules; these molecules have been resolved into atoms, and the atoms into electrons. Tests have concluded that these electrons fill up all space; they exist everywhere.

This is what builds the Universe; this is what everything and everyone including you and I, are made up of, Energy! The director of this energy is your mind. You tell it where to go with your thoughts and feelings.

Electrons form in our body as cells. Each one of these cells possess intelligence; each cell is a living organism. There are a number of electrons revolving around a center of which constitutes an atom. This is how our body is able to work to fight off disease, to build tissue and repair damage, to pump blood around our body and to keep our hearts beating, not to mention the thousands of other jobs these intelligent cells do for us.

We are the overseer of the thoughts we choose and we do this with our free will. We do this with our conscious thoughts. However, there is much more to us than the thoughts we think. We also have a subconscious or subjective mind. We all know our subconscious mind very well and understand this is the part of us that takes over when we have repetitively learned an action. As children we may have learned how to ride a bike or skate or count and read. We did these things repeatedly until our subconscious took over. From that point onwards we could do these things easily without much thought to it. As adults we have taken on so much more and we do tasks daily without a thought as to what actions we need to use to accomplish them. Whether they are small manual jobs or complicated paperwork, or registering numerous telephone numbers. Regardless, the discoveries that have been made into our subconscious is quite amazing, and it is through our subconscious that we are connected to this invincible power each one of us have.

Our Conscious Mind vs. Our Subconscious Mind.

This is the natural design that differentiate between the two: Our conscious mind sets in motion impulses traveling at 120 to 140 mph. The capacity to master an average of 2,000 pieces of data per second. It incorporates only about one sixth of your actual mental capacity.

The subconscious mind has a much larger processing dimension. Its magnitude represents five sixth of your actual mental ability. Long term memory: it programs and keeps records of your past, values and beliefs. The skill to manage thousands of incidents and actions. Its impact delivers 100,000 mph. It can typically process 4,000,000,000 bits of information per second.

This is a breath-taking account of how the subconscious mind works. As we can see in innumerable ways it is more impressive and powerful than our conscious mind. This is where our self image lives, and also where we stockpile all negativity about ourselves. Our subconscious mind functions in every single cell of our body intelligently. This part of our mind is where we have directed it to be; we are living under those old instruction we have impressed upon it from as far back as we can remember.

Our subconscious mind is connected to the Universal Mind, which is also referred to as Our Higher Self, you may say God, the Universe, the Source, Infinite Intelligence, Inner Being or whatever name you can relate to, it is one of the same. This Natural Law governs gravity, the planets and the entire Earth's population, and Earth itself. This law is called the 'Law of Attraction. This law is working with us every moment of our lives, which means, if we are constantly thinking negative thoughts the Law of Attraction reflects those thoughts back to us in situations and circumstances from minute to minute, throughout our lives. Our subconscious does not have the ability to make decisions for us, it does not have will power, it does what it is directed to do from the messages we transmit to it.

By virtue of our being unacquainted to this concept, our active thoughts have given approval to any conflicting ideas from our external world. We allow these negative messages to dictate to us the way our life should develop. Without knowing we can control every circumstance in our lives, we sleepwalk through our lives and often, 'Go with the flow,' so to speak.

The way to change this is by choosing to change our conscious thoughts, by redirecting these thoughts to the vast power of the subconscious mind. New ideas eventually impress the subconscious mind. The subconscious mind does not reject any idea it is fed, it is not bias, it believes everything that you tell it.

We need to get those old thought waves away from the center stage and replace them with new thoughts and positive ideas. We do this with affirmations, visualization and our feelings. And the reason for this is, our subconscious mind needs repetition and the practice of habit. As we now know, all we have ever learned, came from repetition. When we study, our successes originate from those studies and the routine of repeated data we take in. The more we focus on anything in life the more it becomes natural for us to do. This is because our subconscious thrives on repetition which becomes our habits, and once it has been programmed either in a negative way or a positive way it is then set and it will not change until you change the program. Consequently, it is extremely important we use props such as affirmations to repeat strong positive words and thoughts to our deeper self when we are changing our belief system. In the same vein as anything we have learned we repeat our affirmations. We will talk more about this in a later chapter.

Visualization is also very important, this is how visualization works: our thoughts create pictures constantly, when we say something or have a conversation with someone our mind puts out constant pictures to reflect what we are saying, they replicate our thoughts as we speak. We may not always comprehend this, for instance, when someone mentions, "Did you see his old car?" our mind instantly envisions the old car. Therefore, as we focus on what we would like our lives to be, we need to visualize, as clearly as possible, what that will look like when we have it.

This is how powerful our mind is. We have all heard of the *Titanic* and how that wonderful ship was destroyed when it came into collision with an iceberg in 1912. Only 10 percent of the iceberg was above sea level while 90 percent was below. Typically, only one-ninth of a volume of an iceberg is above water while the remaining volume is below water. On a similar account we may perceive our own intellect as being in resemblance to the tip of the iceberg, and our Higher Self being in resemblance to the remaining 90 percent of this unseen part of us. This is our superior part, our creative part. This comes from the Universal Law of Creation.

Just as the icebergs that destroyed the *Titanic* was powerful in its destruction, so can our thoughts be in our lives, but they can also be powerful in a joyous way if we use our thoughts with harmony and love towards our fellow man and ourselves.

We are connected with the Universe and everything in the Universe. This is the unseen part of us. This is the part that shows us the results of our choices. There isn't anything that happens to us out of bad luck, what happens to us is the result of our thoughts, actions and our reactions to any given situation in our lives. We can change any of our circumstances and be connected with our Higher Self through our mind. This is our satellite dish, we send the signal from our conscious thoughts to our subconscious; this is the way we connect. When we understand this clearly we begin to gain control over our own existence.

By impressing our conscious thoughts and transmitting the message clearly to our subconscious with positive thoughts, we will attract the things, people, places and ideal job situations and circumstances we want. By impressing the life that we would love to lead upon our subconscious we replace the negativity in our lives with positive thoughts.

There are thousands of people amongst us that are discovering this and making complete changes to their lives, changes they didn't know were possible. Nevertheless we have to keep in mind, any changes we would like to make have to be in harmony with this Natural Law we live by. This Law will give us all that we want if we do it for not only our benefit, but this must be beneficial to all; everyone and everything. It simply means you must not have harmful thoughts, or bring about ill-natured intentions to others, or our environment. If you do, they will only backfire like a thunderbolt cracking down on you with the most intense explosion, 'what goes around comes around.'

The Law of Attraction has been working since time began. It has been working in your life and mine since we entered this earth. It is exact and never alters. It is reliable, indisputable and unfailing. Our job is to have faith and believe, then to put this into action by changing our thoughts from negative to positive.

Here's an exercise to try:

Find a quiet place, one where you will not be disturbed for 10-15 minutes. Sit in an upright position and close your eyes. Let your body and mind relax. Imagine all your cells actively working throughout your body. See them, thank them. Feel happiness and warmth as you acknowledge all that they do for you. Repeat this exercise daily for the next week. This will help you to start building your positive energy. In the next chapter you will learn how to remove fear from all aspects of your life.

TWO

Changing our thoughts.

"What we achieve inwardly will change outer reality."
Plutarch.

Fear

Negative thoughts are based in fear, but what is fear? Fear is something we manifest from different circumstances; it draws low energy forces. These forces are what we have allowed to enter into our lives. It is a diminished energy vibration which can induce unseen panic. Fear is the toxic forces we have given a green light to enter our lives, and in many cases rule our lives. These unseen forces are what we hold close to ourselves and accordingly, what we give credence to, and then, the Law of Attraction matches whatever we have come to expect.

From the standpoint of fear, life appears to be unstable, threatening and menacing. It seems to be fraught with danger. When people take on this focus, our external world is obliging and therefore bestows to us even greater quantities of this negative data. The Law of Attraction gives you what you give out in energy vibration. This Law is a living law working in our lives, every second. It is not bias, it works with all of our thoughts and actions whether positive or negative, and brings to us corresponding situations and conditions. Consequently, when we live in fear we bring more fearful circumstances and situations to us. The problem is we do not really understand this fear therefore, we do not question it; on that account we let fear rule our lives daily.

If we allow it fear can become agreeable, it becomes comfortable and we become attached to it, and although painful, we give it our permission to run every aspect of our life without having any notion to stop it. Fear is like those old shoes, so comfortable you hate to throw them out no matter how shabby they may become. This fear can live and breathe in us each moment of our lives if we let it. This is why so many people get into deep trouble with drugs, alcohol, sex based on control, anger, eating, shopping and begrudging others amongst many other obsessions. We all suffer some stage of it; we have been given fearful messages throughout our lives. Messages from people who think they are protecting us may lead to fear such as: *"You can drown if you go near the water. Be careful where you walk in the street, the cars may hit you. Don't go near the stove you could get burned."* These are well meaning messages and young children need these warnings but some people literally warn their children so much that everything seems to cry out danger to the child and the child will literally freeze into that danger zone. If children were taught to really understand their own instincts from an early age we wouldn't need to warn them constantly. They would listen to their own feelings of warnings and know in an instant that this feels wrong. *This feels dangerous.* As children, our instincts were sharp. However, some children were inclined to lose these natural impulses initially because they were drowned out at an early age. Instead they made fearful messages an integral part of their attitudes or beliefs: These innumerable messages became their new way of thinking and their instincts submerged far beyond their reach. This doorway to fear based thinking has stayed open throughout most people's lives.

Daily we are drawn to horrific conditions in our world, we are fed constantly with this negative data. Our regular diet is a future filled with doom and gloom. If we choose to believe all of the dogma which builds a wall of fear around us, we will be incapacitated with negativity, never to move forward. Our only hope is through the positive mind, our power is in line with a Natural Law. There is nothing in our external world that can really hurt us if we work with this Natural Law that truly governs us. Negative control is weak external power, but if you think it is strong and take in this frightening communication then what you dread will come about.

The problem is, these messages and this layer of our psyche is so deep within our subconscious we don't even know it's going on. That being the case, we carry on out of sheer ignorance, we become anesthetized and when we are thrown out of gear we haven't a clue that we have been, then yet again, we sabotage our own progress and any breakthrough we may have reached. The only way to change this is by changing our belief system. However, it cannot be healed without recognizing this negativity is there. This is why we have to understand the dynamics that lay behind our thoughts.

Our real work consists in convincing ourselves of the untruthful statements of these erroneous messages we insist on believing. Our first step to overcome this attachment to these fearful messages is awareness. When you become alert to this attachment it becomes an awakening, it is a doorway to change, an opening to your full potential of a life you deserve. But you have to believe you deserve to be rich and happy in every sense of the word. Those of us that are able to face the dread we believe exists in our lives, have come to realize these ominous words that we tell ourselves constantly, in truth, hold no ominous content of fear at all. And when we face this we have stepped over the threshold of fear and have activated guidance and protection, and to our benefit we have attracted an undeniable safety net. We feel it and welcome it in every part of our system. For some, feeling truly guided and protected takes place for the first time in their entire existence on this Earth. Before this, they have felt alone. The people that were supposed to have loved, guided and protected them were not there, and so this is truly a wonderful revelation.

Indeed, to believe and to trust in this loving Universe are the first requirements to become the Master of Self. To start on the journey to empowerment.

There is a prerequisite to become the 'Master of our Mind' and it calls for us to substitute each negative thought for a positive one. This is a necessity, it is our first obligation of love to ourselves. We must love ourselves to transmit this new data. We deserve all the good life has in store for us, so it is vital we convey this important message to our psyche clearly.

This may sound like a startling task. One that may seem way too bothersome to monitor each thought that rolls by. Therefore, through this book we will help you to understand the easy way to do this, so don't get put off with this idea of changing your thoughts. It will be the most powerful thing you've ever done, and the best thing you will ever do.

This is how we evolve from this minute onwards, by this new process of monitoring our thoughts as often as we can catch them. We have thousands of thoughts whirling through our minds like cyclones moving at destructively high speeds which may nullify any positive energy we have digested, and so it is not possible to catch every thought. Regardless, let us look at it more that you are guiding your thoughts than stopping and changing them outright. We can start to replace as many as possible by being aware of where our thoughts are going. When we catch ourselves dwelling on a negative thought we can stop ourselves from 'going there' to the place that weakens us. In this manner we are tipping the balance from negativity and stepping into the positive energy field.

Some people may become intimidated by all the negative thoughts they have. They fear they may be bringing severe consequences for all the negative thoughts they think. But it has been scientifically proven that a positive thought holds tremendous power that negative thoughts do not. The sooner you are aware of the negative thoughts that are passing through your mind the sooner you can dismiss the power they hold. Even after a negative thought has entered your mind there is a time delay and you can catch the thought and reject it. When you replace it with a positive thought you have activated a powerful part of you, the part that dominates the weaknesses in your psyche.

Feelings are a great help in this process as feelings are our first real indication we are on a low energy thought system. When we are positive we feel optimistic, we feel happy, we feel light, weightless, we give our smiles away effortlessly; we have no intention to hurt each other, we give our love easily and this love returns to us. We all need to pay close attention to our feelings. This is our true self, our Higher Self, telling us whether or not we are being harsh to ourselves and others.

Feelings are our intentions to our fellow humans as well as to ourselves. If we feel hurt it shows in the grate in our gut, this is our insight, our deeper self, telling us we are using our forces in a negative way. If we feel angry, we feel it in the whole of our being and sometimes we give it back in hurtful words, hurting other people. This only backfires and the impact is like a searing lather pouring back down onto us. So you see, to give hurtful words one will suffer the consequences eventually. The Law of Attraction works in the positive and the negative, it does not discriminate. It gives back to you what you give out.

We are born with many characteristics. These characteristics have been collected along the way. Your temperament, disposition, idiosyncrasies, traits, integrity, in fact, all of your personality reflect your purpose or goal in life. These different parts of us are the parts that become angry, intimidated, hurt, jealous, sensitive, suspicious, and then happy, loving, considerate, tactful and affectionate amongst many others, so as you can see, we have a lot of different aspects of ourselves to deal with. The problem is, we have to figure out what part of our personality is at the fore of our circumstance at any given moment. What role are we playing today? When we decide we would prefer to live with our compassionate side we begin to exile those unwanted parts of us. However, they will not want to leave and will keep returning, accordingly it is our duty to ourselves not to let them overpower us. We do this by replacing the old invalid belief system with the full intention of placing our compassionate side on the stage of our life as often as we think about it.

Changing our thoughts compel us to be responsible to ourselves and also other people.

Each part of our personality plays its own role in our lives. Have you said or done something that made you say, *"Why did I do that?"* Or, *"What was I thinking when I did that?"* We all have been there because we have allowed different parts of our personality to take control at the particular time it happened. It's similar to an aircraft being on autopilot, you sit back and let it take the controls for you. The difference is, with your aircraft you haven't a clue as to where it will navigate to, therefore, you cannot avoid anything you may collide with.

We have never really learned that there is a stronger side to us, a part that is very powerful. This part has always been there waiting in the wings to assist us, eager for us to take full sovereignty over the weaker parts of our personality. Once we come to this understanding we realize it is time to take dominion over negative data, the part we had previously given permission to take control over us.

Our objective on Earth is to take our authority back and we do this by changing our thoughts. We need to make sure we don't give the undesirable part of our personality center stage. When we take our power back and crush those negative thoughts we send the uninvited part of our personality away, where it belongs—from the center stage.

I often call it the old Pamela, and think, *"That's the old Pamela trying once again to gain the upper hand."* I smile to myself and try to take full control, but sometimes that old Pamela and I have a struggle. The problem is, we have become used to "Joining in," we have gotten used to agreeing with people, and on that account our old self will join in the negative gossip, that part of our personality relishes in what it perceives as enjoyment in judging other people. Yet we must remember while we are doing this we activate the third law of motion, which is, 'For every action there is an equal and opposite reaction.' The person we are judging, is judging us also. Therefore, whatever negative statements we say about another person will be said about us. This is the law, it is exact, it always gives to us what we give out. This is what we attract to ourselves.

Actually when we do start to observe our thoughts, it is surprising where they go from minute to minute. Do you realize when we have a conversation with other people it is only a matter of minutes before negativity enters into it? With some people it is really difficult to turn the conversation around. When you begin to monitor your conversation with others you begin to see how much negativity we really do live with. We are so attached to it we seem to function in it without a thought. Regardless, we can change this. It is not impossible. There is nothing impossible within this Natural Law of Change.

Just keep in mind we are all alike. We are all part of the one whole. We are not so out of the ordinary as we may think. Our struggles are similar to the seven billion people we share this earth with. We are struggling with our attachments to our former convictions; we are not happy with our trials and tribulations, we don't understand our adversities in life and we don't get why they have to be repeated so often. Now is the time to find those answers and see the major changes actually take form in your life.

Essentially when we come upon this journey we find it is an exciting time and full of disclosure and fun.

Positive vs. Negative.

Once we realize there is a greater power and it comes from an indisputable law, and it rules us with absolute preciseness, then we come to realize also that we have a loving partner with us and has been with us from birth. This Natural Law works in our lives constantly, lovingly and like any good parent, it only wants what is best for us, it is always there, although we have been unconscious to this law, it has always been cheering us on.

When we live in negativity we try to exist by ourselves. We distance ourselves from our fellow humans, this drains us of vitality, and we feel confused and alone. We give in to any opposing messages, spiraling downwards like a broken ship in a storm. We lose our ability to feel the deeper meaning in life, everything feels foreign, unfamiliar and strange. This limits any self development.

When we live with positive thoughts we evolve. We come to know we are not alone. We begin to see a loving Universe that will cherish us unquestionably, bringing forth joy and happiness by giving us all that we wish for. Our life changes in ways we could not imagine and we begin to see our own talents and creativity. We marvel at the miracle of life. Each day we wake is a day of blessing.

Changing our views.

At first it is a struggle, remember that this negative energy has been governing your entire thought system for the majority of your life. It's been given full reign to wield the scepter. Now you are taking it back. It will not want to give up so easily. Your part is to realize you have the power of the Infinite Intelligence, God, the Universe... always with you. This is the most powerful influence ever known. Each time you catch a negative thought and then reject it, the Universe sees it as a victory, because each time we step on the stairway of confidence we uplift not only ourselves but also others, collectively. This is how powerful each one of us are. When we lift ourselves to this higher energy field we do it not only for us, but for every other living person. We are all part of the one whole. This is how important your job is. This is how important we all are individually.

Although it may seem farfetched to say that each of us can uplift the remaining population of this world, we absolutely can. I found this quite unbelievable at first. How can little me uplift anyone by my actions or thoughts? (at that time I didn't understand my power—that I am much more than a little me!) Consider that it may seem as if we live in our own world with our own things around us; the people we surround ourselves with also live in their world with their things. But in our interactions with people we develop our views, those people influence us, and also our views influence their views. If we do something unusual to 'the mainstream views' of our world we are looked upon as being odd, different. And because the world doesn't accept us, we feel alone, we feel forsaken, rejected, an outcast, we feel reduced. This is because in the core of our being we strive for acceptance. We strive for acceptance because we have a bond with one another for the greater good. This tells us how much we need each other. This connection becomes more apparent when we watch someone that is humiliated, we feel their embarrassment. When we see someone that is suffering we feel their pain, when we see someone that is angry with another person, we feel their fear. This is the essence of our true nature by virtue of the attachment we have with each other. Despite this fact, approval from our external world is what we seek to aspire to, and yet, our external world cannot give us the answers we need, the power or the love. If we cannot help ourselves through this external world we cannot help one another, and although we do not identify with this idea, nevertheless, we feel this loss deep within our psyche.

We then feed into negative thoughts which impacts the world with more negativity. We pass it on, not intentionally, as we haven't recognized our union with the whole. Nevertheless, these vibrations of negativity are sent out impacting more negative social views. The more low energy that is repeatedly sent out into the world the more people are kept where they are, including ourselves, if we stay in this negative energy field.

Another way we concur with negativity is by constantly bringing our focus on a negative circumstance or situation. It may be that the circumstance or situation will pass on from this world, but when we cling to an undesirable situation we give that particular situation energy. Because it now has this energy, the situation is able to stay. If we were to let that situation go by taking our thoughts away from it, that particular situation will leave, it cannot stay without energy. Everything is made up of energy.

When a fluctuation of high energy is delivered it uplifts humanity. The teachings of Jesus Christ, Buddha, Lord Krishna, Mohammed amongst many others were testaments to this. They all calibrated at very high energy frequencies and their impact on the world was embraced in love, acceptance and compassion for their fellow man. They uplifted people far and wide with inner peace and high energy frequency, and still do.

Although we feel our thoughts are our own, we do have some responsibility to our world to make a change. Each one of us that makes the change from negative to positive brings us all towards the wonderful life we are meant to live. The great teachers that went before us knew this, taught this, wanted this for us and now more than ever, since time began, we are feeling this. We have evolved to this point, we are no longer just able to 'go with the flow.' We are not happy to just, 'take our lot in life,' after all it wasn't our lot to begin with. We are coming to an awakening and it is a wonderful feeling. Our perceptions are much sharper than our ancestors' ever were. We are curious and questioning our life and mortality in ways we have never thought to do before. We are no longer willing to just survive.

To change our lives and bring invincible powers to us we have to understand all power comes from within us and not from the world we live in. The world we live in is external power. This power is weak and unreliable. External power comes from man. It resembles plastic that appears to be leather, it may look the same but it is not durable, or long lasting. Worldly power that comes from greed is fleeting and those that have it are never completely happy. Power from within oneself is connected strongly to Infinite Power, it is resistant to outside influences. It comes from a compassionate place within us, a place that wants not only great possibilities for us but for everyone else also.

What you see in your life at this moment reflects your past thoughts. If you are living in constant negativity it means your predominant thoughts are negative. When we come to an understanding of the wisdom from within we will see the true possibilities of our life.

The more we change our thoughts, the more we see results, the more we believe in this natural power. This is a gift of infinite wisdom which is ours to use constructively and creatively from a loving Universe. It is a gift of Infinite Love. When we come to understand this we take possession of what is ours and we see possibilities beyond what we have ever dreamed of enter our lives, and the Universe rejoices.

When I first came upon this journey I came to understand that if we have strong expectations that dominate our thoughts they are certainly going to manifest whether good or bad. This is how it works and how powerful we are. This little scenario happened to me prior to all of this knowledge I have now come to know.

Years ago when I had appointments at my doctor's office there were only parking for four cars, and two of those parking spaces were for the two doctors. Everyone else had limited parking on the street. I didn't think too much about parking; every time I went to the doctors I was able to park in one of those two spots. I never considered that I wouldn't find one empty. I just drove up to those two parking spaces and either there was one empty or someone was just pulling out. My husband complained, he always had to find parking, it was always a bother. I remember saying that I always parked without a problem. It wasn't until I learned about The Law of Attraction that I understood through my intention, at that time, there would always be a parking space available for me, and there always was. I expected it.

This is how it works. You have to intend it. You have to claim this as your own. Many people have what we would perceive as good fortune because unconsciously they intend it to be. However it is not luck or fortune. It is a Natural Law that is in place. It gives us what we want. We just have to be on the page of receiving it, and then we can, without a doubt, expect it.

The problem is most people don't expect much in life. They place their wants and desires last. They feel that everyone else should come before them, as if they have no rights. They never consider their needs or that they can actually intend good things to happen to them. They would never contemplate this idea of intending something for themselves believing that it couldn't possibly happen for them. I am here to say you deserve anything in life which would make you happy. Intend it and expect it. You are no less deserving than anyone else on this earth.

These intentions have to be in harmony with this law. It is the only way it works to our advantage.

The problem we have is because we believe we don't deserve positive experiences or things in our life, our constant complaints about what we don't have, keep us in this negative field. We talk constantly about what we don't want or don't have or we become upset or jealous with those that have the things we want that these complaints constantly echo in our head. Unfortunately this is what manifests into our lives. What we ceaselessly think about or complain about eventually manifests in our lives. It is law.

When I began to understand how we can control our thoughts and situations I used it in meetings, with my job, and quite a few circumstances. I did this with the idea of not only a good outcome for me but a good outcome for all who were involved in my work duties. If we do this with honesty then we reap wonderful outcomes.

Difficult managers and people are no longer difficult and situations just smooth out. This is where it becomes fun. As long as your intentions are with a good heart it is amazing what can happen. It is as if someone has gone before you and smoothed everything out! And of course someone has, our loving Universe.

Life gives us a choice which starts with the question, *'Do we want all the joy life would like to give to usm or are we comfortable to stay where we are, wandering aimlessly, never knowing what will be thrown in our way?'*

Throughout this chapter we have talked about fear and controlling the negative thoughts and conversations you have on a daily basis. This exercise will be a simple and fun one.

1) Choose something that makes you feel happy when you think about it. It could be anything. An experience, a song, a person, place. It needs to be

something that instantly changes your feelings from negative to positive.

2) Make a mental note each time a negative thought comes to you and replace it with the positive thought. Really focus on the feelings you have when you substitute these thoughts.

3) Be aware and present in each conversation you have. Your goal is to refrain from adding to the negative ones and offering positive contribution to each conversation. Note: This will be difficult at first, The more you build the habit of offering kind words and positive solutions the higher your energy field becomes. You will begin to attract more positive experiences in your life.

4) Choose a day to write down all the negative thoughts and conversations you have from the beginning of the day to the end. Make sure you date it. Then repeat the exercise in three weeks and compare the results. Then repeat it again in another three weeks and compare the results. You will see that the negative experiences will drastically diminish as you take control of your thinking.

In business, W. T used this natural law and in a very short time, he did wonders, W. T gives to you hands on ways and situations he used to bring powerful energy to his business which quickly got results, please read on...

THREE

If you do the same thing all the time why do you expect different results?

"To be yourself in a world that is constantly trying to make you something else is the greatest accomplishment."
Ralph Waldo Emerson (1803-1882)

It is easy to fall into a routine, to get comfortable, to do the status quo. We all do it or have done it. There are many excuses to support this behavior or attitude. The one thing that you fail to do is to ask why things are not changing or improving. I remember seeing others getting ahead and saying *"they are so lucky"* or *"their parents help them out."* But then I asked myself, what are they really doing differently from me? They're probably making the same money as me, have the same education and skills as me. So what is it that they are doing differently from me?

I found out the answer is everything! They see life as full of opportunities and they see themselves as entitled to take advantage of those opportunities. They are willing to take chances, to try something without any guarantee of success.

They are not waiting to see if someone else will succeed at it first. They are not waiting for an opportunity to land in their lap.

They are thinking things through, adding up the risks and rewards, and making a calculated determination of how to proceed. They do what I was afraid to do. They take charge and move when others are talking themselves out of moving. They look at the result of their last adventure and see what they can do different this time. They learn from their failures and from their accomplishments. They build confidence with each new opportunity they tackle and they never live the same day twice.

My story...

I was working in a job I loved as the production manager, you will find out in another chapter how I became a production manager. I was having fun every day and was working really hard. I had a hard working group of guys who loved what they did and were always there for me when I needed them. I treated them well, pushed them when needed, but I also knew how to relax and reward them. The company was very busy and the product was in high demand.

Then the economy tanked. The company went bankrupt.

I was fortunate to be a key player at the company and was directly involved in bringing the company back to life with an investment firm. There were many meetings and talks with guys in fancy pants and shoes. I kept confident through the whole process that the company would come back to life and I would be a key part of it. The company, which previously had a minority owner at the helm, was bought out by an investment firm.

To my surprise they were not going to pay me what I was making before. They also changed my job asking me to go into sales, even though I had little prior experience.

The deal was to help bring the company back to profit, then there would be rewards. I understood this and accepted this. There were now new owners, that had invested money so we could get it started again. I worked hard and long hours for straight salary (no commissions). I had a lot of pressure to bring results, find customers, win back former customers and expand the market with a new strategy. After a year and a half of building up the customer base we were on stable ground and breaking even. As we started to make money and increase the bottom line I felt it was time to ask for a raise. I was told: *"Not right now, we need to see how the next few months go,"* so I waited patiently. After a few more months of strong sales, I asked again. Each time we were doing as good as the last month or a bit better but always the answer was the same. *"Just hold on, be patient and we will look after you."* But I was not making enough money. I was no longer able to live the lifestyle which I had become accustomed to. I also noticed that the executives were buying cars and going on trips. The company had enough money to pay them a good salary. I had two options: Keep doing what I'd been doing and hope something will change, or take a different approach. So I decided to focus on getting a better job that paid more money and had more incentives, but was still as fun as the last job.

I didn't know what exactly I would do or where I would find the job. As soon as I started focusing on finding a new job and improving my situation, options started pouring in. At that time, I didn't know if they were always there and I hadn't noticed, or if I drew them to me. It doesn't really matter. What matters is that I decided to change the way I did things and within a few months I was working at a better company for more money and the conditions were better than ever!

You can do the same thing with your life. You don't have to do what everyone else is doing. Everyone else isn't living your life. Everyone else doesn't have to live with the choices you make. You have to be in control of your life and be excited to live your life.

You have to realize you can set the rules for you. You can decide how you want to live. You can decide how much fun you want to have. You can determine how much money you want to have; to spend. In order to do this you first have to identify what is stopping you, or has stopped you to this point? This is a question I had to ask myself before I could do what I was able to do.

The answer I found, was me, or more precisely, my mind. The way I think, how I look at things, how I react to things, what I expected out of life; these are the factors that control my thought process. Maybe you never thought that doing things differently could bring different results. Maybe you think you are just not working hard enough or you are not trying hard enough. Maybe you've been thinking you are just unlucky. The point is, you need to change how you think. This may be the hardest first step you will take in your life, I know it was for me. Those who see opportunity usually have great lives or are doing better than average at minimum. You need to get on this road, to travel in this circle.

It's never too late to change. See things through new eyes. Question what you have been taught and see if it still fits. Try new things. Your mind needs to be open to new possibilities. You cannot have a preconceived conclusion. Explore, be adventurous, be brave, be curious, walk through the door when it opens.

So now comes the question: If you are not moving forward where are you going?

Doing the same thing all the time will leave you in the same place year after year, and you will watch all those around you move on to new jobs, better houses and nicer cars, all while you grow more frustrated with your life. I was there. I watched everyone take chances and leave for better opportunities all while I was staying in the same job, comfortably wondering why I wasn't moving forward. You see life is a process of growth and movement. Nothing stays the same for long periods of time. The clothes you were wearing 10 years ago are not the ones you wear now. Thinking about where you want to be, is the first step in breaking the cycle and getting out of your safety zone. You are meant to move forward, to have a better life today than you had yesterday. What I have found is, life will always challenge you, there will be setbacks, but you must learn from them. You must learn what you can do differently the next time to change the result. I had to sit down with a piece of paper and write out how I could improve my situation, what I had learned from the experience I had at my previous job. I had to do this to understand how I could do things differently for the next opportunity that came my way. It was the only way to make sure I changed my thinking. I had to understand *how* I thought before I could change the *way* I thought.

It is not easy to dissect yourself in this way nor is it comfortable, but it is a must if you want to grow and move forward. You need to have a picture of how your life will look. You need to hold that picture in your mind and focus on it. You can't move forward if you don't know where you are trying to go. You can't move forward if you are not willing to learn. You need to grow your understanding of the possibilities around you.

Be a student of life. Never stop learning. Be a sponge. Soak up the knowledge whenever you come across it. Learn how to use it to improve your life. Believe that you can do anything you focus on.

Have you ever wondered why so many people can succeed at things that look impossible?

This is something that used to amaze me. How did Jay-Z go from a drug dealer to partying with Warren Buffett? How did Barack Obama become President of the United States of America? How did Oprah achieve what she did, when she did, in the field she was working in? In their mind it wasn't impossible. In their mind they could see the end result. They focused on the end result and didn't get lost in the 'how.' They only see and focused on the 'what,' the outcome. This is the advantage that others have. Some have better focus on the end result to bring them success. Some have larger ideas to bring them success, but all have one thing in common. There is one thing that sets them apart in their field, one thing that stands out above all. It is not talent, luck, or circumstance. It is the belief that they deserve to succeed. The passion, dedication and focus on the end result. They see things in a new light. They see all the possibilities, all the rewards and focus on those. *The risks are not even worth spending their valuable mental energy on.* There is little fear, and what does exist is ignored. This spoke to me, changing my belief in what I could do. It was like a light went off in my head. I realized I am the only one that can stand in my way. I set the bar and only I can raise it. I came to the conclusion and belief that there is nothing, no matter what, who, or where that can stand in my way; I only have to convince myself that I can succeed, then move and take the actions which are necessary to succeed.

I realized at some point they have learned to retrain their brain to bring the end result to them. They are not afraid to go for what they want. They are not afraid to try. They see their future before they start and chase that future until it is in the now. I also realized this change, this endeavor comes with almost zero cost.

I was given a book from my Mom, I bought a few books, and read some for free on the internet. This was more of an investment of time and belief. I was investing in myself to bring financial gain, mental strength, and confidence into my life on my terms and for my own happiness.

What I had to understand is that every cause has an effect. I read in the 'Master Key,' that your predominate thoughts attract those things into your life like a magnet attracts metal. We have positive and negative thoughts. The result of your thoughts will show up in your life, in the now, as your standard of living or your current living conditions. I also learned that my conscious thoughts will influence my subconscious thoughts. I needed to focus on what I wanted to think about. Nothing but these thoughts can be on my mind. Positive thinking is a discipline that takes training and dedication.

To control your thoughts is to control the effect. So this is how my quest for change began. I had to know what I was thinking about. I had to focus on achieving my goals and not get side tracked. I had to practice concentrating on the end result. Most of all, I had to learn new things.

This is the work that must be done to really champion "doing things differently" It is not just words, it is action, it is consistency. This is based on the laws of science and is measurable. This knowledge is being used all the time by many successful people in many industries. Some people do not know what it is; they don't have to think about it, they are already wired this way. The rest of us have to train our brain to think this way. We have to make a conscious effort to focus our thought on the goal. We have to believe that we can achieve whatever we put our mind to.

You will see the fruits of this labor in your life almost instantly. It is amazing how changing the way you think even in the smallest way will bring noticeable results quickly. You will become excited about it and want to learn more so that you can get better at it and enjoy bigger triumphs. Even though it sounds crazy, what you think about is attracting more of the same into your life, whether you believe it or not.

Know that this is true, use this tool and knowledge to gain the advantage in the now.

It is time to start practicing thinking about what you want your life to look like. To see in your mind's eye all the possibilities of your hidden potential. To see your future self and future experiences. In the beginning of this chapter I talked about writing down what I wanted my life to look like. You need to make this list now. Write in detail the type of things you want to have and to experience. In a later chapter we will do a visualization exercise using this list but for now I want you to create this list and read it each night before you go to bed.

Re-read this chapter in one week and ask yourself,

If you do the same thing all the time why do you expect different results?

Back to Pamela: Find out how every thought you make affects the conditions in your life!

FOUR

Cause and Effect

*"Every thought is a cause and every condition is an effect.
Change your thoughts and you change your destiny."*
Joseph Murphy (1898-1981)

Business and Cause and Effect

Most of us are familiar with Wal-Mart and its success. We may think the success is due to very low prices, although that certainly is a great pull for many of us to visit the store, however, there is a far more compelling reason that justifies such ongoing success than what meets the eye.

When *Sam Walton*, the founder of Wal-Mart, started this colossus business, he wanted it to be warm with a humane energy. He trained his employees to be accommodating, warm, and energetic. In fact *Sam Walton* adequately developed a place of goodwill to both workers and the consumer which not only increased the human value of the experience of the consumer, but in turn produced gross sales.

This came from a man who placed the idea of compassion first with a family feeling added.

Recently on the TV there was a British period television drama called, *'Mr. Selfridge.'* Harry Selfridge started one of the first major department stores in London, England, in the 1900's. An American flamboyant visionary, Harry Selfridge was much in likeness with his later counterpart, *Sam Walton,* due to his compassion for his workers and his perception that positive feelings, given out to the customers, determined purchases.

This is a prominent quality in successful businesses and companies. When employees feel nurtured and valued, they respond with smiles and extend care to the people they deal with in the company. Businesses that are cold and calculating; that are only interested in the gross sales and not the employees or customers—become the businesses or companies which eventually fail. These establishments have low energy patterns. They are impersonal. They are running with no particular feelings for anyone and eventually they self destruct.

Wal-Mart and Selfridges are both prominent department stores, one opened in 1909 and the other opened in 1962, both are still going strong today. Their owners, *Harry Selfridge* and *Sam Walton,* managed to attain great achievements by using benevolence towards the people they dealt with and towards their employee's.

High employment turnover is a great indicator of low energy levels in the workplace. Detached, insensitive employers make the mistake of cutting back on staff which produces miserable employees with low energy fields. They are not valued, which they depict in their nonchalant faces and unwelcome feelings towards the consumer.

Low energy fields continually reduce companies, businesses and careers; in fact any line of profession or occupation when it can be avoided by correlating with high energy which is harmonious with natural laws.

The *'Master Key System'* is still used by many wealthy businessmen today. There are millionaires and billionaires that have followed the teachings of *Charles Haanel*. One of the chief principles of his teaching is about how cause and effect work in our businesses and our lives.

Cause is the result transpiring from an effect. In other words, if a person doing a deal decides he or she should profit from defective goods, the money they receive for the imperfect goods will lose value rapidly, or the business itself will depreciate amongst many other things that could possibly happen from a sinister deal. This is a natural law. It is the same law that rules gravitation, electricity, the internet, the planets and the universe. This same law governs you and I.

Consequently, when you have the effect you didn't wish for, instead of cursing somebody off or doing 'the blame game,' think of what cause you may have taken to be given the undesired effect. This gives to some investigation on your part. *We often do things habitual in life and we find it difficult to locate the reason why this happened because we instantly look at the effect for the answer and are blinded to the initial cause.* However, once we start to sift through our memory and remind ourselves what the cause could possibly be, we may realize why this so called bad luck happened. (By the way there isn't such a thing as bad luck, only bad choices on our part.)

Companies that are in the competitive game without any thought to harmony will find it is an uphill battle all the way. Those that succeed in competition will only reign for a time and fail. Many companies that seem to be on top are struggling and wasting money trying to stay on top. Companies that enhance the people who are working for them and the people they serve are the ones that thrive. It is as simple as that. Cause and effect work with a natural law. If a person causes harm to another then the effect is disastrous to them and so this same law also rules business.

We need money to survive and money is our means to happiness but only if it is used in accordance with this law. Any selfish deed done without benevolence to the people one is dealing with, will not be prosperous or beneficial in any way to its owner.

To secure the effect we desire we are to be in tune with our thoughts. This is difficult but can be done. There are many teachers who will warn the only way a businessman can really succeed is with honesty and with harmony towards his fellow man. Without this he may succeed for a time but in the end all will be lost.

We have to search our own actions and not other people's behavior or influence, when something goes wrong in our lives. This way we can figure out the reason why undesirable moments occur in our life and possibly avoid it the next time.

This method of inductive reasoning has been the method of studying nature, the planets and man. This is what brought science and physics to the conclusion that a law so unique, so mighty and powerful, is the same law that rules us. One of the wonderful principles of this law is we can, in fact, control our own lives by controlling the way we think, which in turn controls the way we live, which in turn controls our environment. All we have to do is be in tune with this law.

If we understand an effect is the conclusion from a direction we have given at some point in our lives, we then begin to understand how this law works. We then can conclude that it isn't just the product of a hollow irrational force in our work or our business that just happened for no particular reason. This law is in operation in every moment of our lives. We are the ones who direct it. We have the power to bring this unforeseen circumstance into our lives so we then must deal with the consequence.

Increase

You must intend to give equal material for the price you want or give the rightful price equal to the material you wish for, (this includes those of you who pay the people who work for you.) You must see that you give them a use value proportionate to the cash value you are making, which means you pay the people the cash value they are worth. It doesn't mean you give all your profits away, you could not run a business with that method; it means you give them equal value for the work they do. Regardless, this is good news because when you run your business in a well balanced way you give increase, which is harmonious with Natural Law. If you follow these natural laws you will not only succeed in your business but your business will flourish.

There is a warning about business and cause and effect which is to be vigilant over the temptation to pursue power over other people, or to rule over another for the lust of power. To fall to this temptation is to risk losing all you have struggled for. Remember this is an infallible law and it is indisputable and unfailing and is with us every minute of our lives.

It is important we refer to the law of cause and effect through each decision of our lives on every level whether it be a small decision or to a level of extreme importance.

Throughout time it has been the mistake of individuals, our communities, society, governments and beyond to deduct a conclusion from the effects and ignore the cause. Natural Law reverses this. *It reveals to us that we are to examine the cause first and this is where the answers lay to all of our problems.*

Once the cause has been dissected then there isn't such a sting left behind by any given situation. We begin to understand the patterns of our behaviors and know those situations which we should avoid and learn from.

Life is changing, we are coming closer to the truth of life each day. The day will be gone when we sit back while other men use their forces to pursue their influence over us.

A Virtuous Way to Cause and Effect

Mahatma Ghandi, Martin Luther King, Nelson Mandela and Mother Teresa are symbols of the truth. Each have demonstrated great power to bring man freedom through cause and effect. They did this in peace, they used power against force which brought Empires to crumble before them, laws were changed and century old ideas were cast away.

They understood when we put force into a situation then we actually help keep the situation alive—our magnitude of energy forms together and keeps those conditions or circumstances alight. It is like throwing gas on a fire hoping it will go out.

When people get together and work towards a goal, then thought is strengthened collectively and energy becomes powerful, either with good or bad. So when accumulated thought is angry, it is negative and it can only bring more negative circumstances to the situation we may be fighting. This is why demonstrations of violence do not win. This is what these people understood. *They taught it and won because they knew force was no match against power.*

Have you ever argued with a person that resisted the argument by staying calm? It dissipates because it's like arguing with yourself—you try to keep this negative energy alive but it is battling against a wall and it cannot move forward. If you think you have won you are only deceiving yourself. The force of energy will only turn back on you, it will not touch the person that is peaceful, because the soul of the person, at that moment, is more powerful than yours. No matter what the picture may look like to you.

Anger comes from fear and fear produces pain and powerlessness. A person who is peaceful in any situation draws empowerment to themselves through the positive energy field that surrounds them in the moment.

This is how we change situations by being positive. This is the way we will come to see the effects of great changes to our world, by understanding the cause we impressed upon conditions first and foremost.

So if we want to live in a peaceful world we must be peaceful, if we want to live in a loving world we must choose love. When we do this we will see effects of ultimate joy.

For this exercise, take time to reflect on your past events. Think about the cause and effect, Ask yourself the following questions:

What caused the outcome?

What caused the cause that led to the outcome?

Ask the question again and again until you drill down to the root.

For example, a lack of money may be because one feels they are not paid enough. They should be making $100,000 instead of $50,000. Further investigation may lead to the realization that the skills one possesses are not that of a $100,000 earner. In other words, the mindset of the belief that one doesn't possess the skills needed is stopping them from manifesting the $100,000 they desire. They must believe they have the skills the $100,000 earner has. So now ask the question again and one may realize that a $100,000 earner also invested time, money and belief into the skills they need which go beyond the hours of the 9-5 job. The $50,000 earner did not, so the root cause now appears to be how one uses their time off from the job hours. But ask the question again and one will find the $100,000 earners mindset is not the same as the $50,000 earner. The

$100,000 earner is never satisfied with what they know or where they are at. They invest their time into things that will make them more valuable. So the true root cause for the $50,000 earner is in how they value themselves and their time.

Try this and have fun with it. You will discover some valuable lessons, you may notice a constant theme in your wins and losses.

W.T will take this a little further and show you how to focus daily on the desired life you would prefer to see.

FIVE

Every Day I Drink The Coffee!!!

*"The person who sends out positive thoughts
activates the world around him positively and
draws back to him positive results."*
Dr. Norman Vincent Peale (1898-1993)

Have you ever heard someone say *"Wake up and smell the coffee!"?* I don't just smell it, I drink the coffee. I enjoy a nice cup before starting my day. I wake up and I say in my head all the things I am grateful for that day and all the things I will be grateful for. I get ready for another awesome day and before leaving the house I drink the coffee. I am aware today is unwritten and I need to be ready for a new adventure. I know there may be new things for me to learn today, new experiences to have. I know I have to 'wake up and smell the coffee!' So I don't miss out on something that could benefit me or at least make my life more interesting. The thing you have to do in life is to enjoy life. Take time to enjoy the coffee, slow down and take in the moment.

I'm talking about the moment every morning when the day is new and the start is fresh. You haven't had to make a big decision yet even if one is pending. You haven't started to worry about deadlines and demands yet. This is the moment you need to take for yourself, if you haven't to date, it is time to start. Before you worry about what the day has in store or what big task you have to do, you should take time to drink the coffee. Sit down, relax, watch something or read something but make it your time. It is not your employer's time, or your kids time, or your spouse's time, it is your time. It might be the only time you truly have to yourself each day. Own it. Make it part of your routine. Make sure you keep this time for you and don't let anyone interrupt it. Savor it.

I drink the coffee, I look forward to finding out new things I can use later on. Maybe not this week or this month, maybe not this quarter or this fiscal year, but I have new knowledge in my back pocket to use when needed. This is one way successful people keep the advantage over others. They are never satisfied with what they know. They are always looking to improve, to stay ahead of everyone. Improving yourself is one of the ways to get ahead of those in front of you. This is one of the main reasons you are reading this. You need to gain the advantage by learning more things than others' know. You save it, hold onto it until it is useful. Wake up and smell the coffee, it will open your eyes, but drinking the coffee will make you alert. You will be ready for whatever comes next. Being prepared for what comes next is invaluable. Being able to step up to the plate in a time of need will make all your preparation worthwhile.

The key is to know what you are trying to accomplish and concentrating on it.

My story chapter 98 part 17... I remember being tired after a long day at work and wanting to watch T.V but my wife had signed up for a 3-night webinar. I had promised her I would watch it with her. It sounded like a good idea a week ago but now I was tired and I didn't want to be bothered. She sat down to watch the webinar without me. Suddenly, I smelled the coffee! I realized that I was going to miss out on a chance to add to my knowledge. This was exactly what I was talking about to my kids and I was going to miss out! I decided to drink the coffee, I was amazed at the things I was learning and was happy to take the webinar. It was 2 hours for three nights with homework but it was worth it. It taught me another way to invest money. I couldn't go out and start doing it immediately after completing the 3 night webinar but I was on a new road of understanding. It came with access to a virtual trade site, and a course manual that was even better than the webinar so we were able to gain a better understanding of what we had learned. If I had not watched the webinar I would have missed out, never able to take advantage of this avenue to grow my money.

This is just one example of how people use their time. Some people read many books on a subject they are interested in, others take courses and seminars, others do nothing, just watch T.V and wait for something to happen for them. You need to drink the coffee and get the knowledge whenever it comes your way. Now I am not talking about constantly learning new things every day. Nor am I talking about gaining information about everything under the sun. Sometimes you can let the answers flow to you. Let the knowledge find you. You just have to be ready for it when it comes your way. There is a reason the webinar came to me. I was looking for ways to increase my money so I could invest in real estate. I wanted to do my first deal with my own money to gain a better understanding of the whole game before I started using investors' money. I needed to understand how I would be able to pay them interest and principal when needed. I didn't have enough money built up to buy a 3-unit place, then the info came to me of a way to turn small amounts of money into bigger amounts of money. I had my eyes open, I saw the knowledge when it presented itself.

You can draw the things you need to you by focusing on the end result. It will always bring to you what you need but you have to focus and stick to the routine. You have to be attentive and drink the coffee whenever you have the chance. Everything I have learned has come from a need. When the need is strong I keep thinking about it until I have a way to fill that need then I move on to the next need. Each day is a new day and I come one day closer to fulfilling the need at hand. This is important to know and be aware of. Smelling the coffee is only part of the answer. You have to *drink* the coffee if you really want to satisfy the need.

It's all about taking action. Action speaks louder than words right? So this is what we do:

1, Identify a need.
2, Look for the solution.
3, Take action.

Drinking the coffee is taking action. When you play chess you look at the pieces on the board, you think ahead to what pieces you want to take out, then you figure out how you can play your pieces to get the result you want while anticipating what your opponent will play. After all that planning, it is time to move your piece. This is how you plan your game in football, this is how you should plan your life. Identify your needs, realize you can change the game and move your pieces how you want in life. Get ready for the answers and be alert. Don't take anything for granted. Things happen because you put something in motion at some point in time to bring you to the now that you are in. If you were seeking a better cup of coffee at some point in your life and a cup comes along unexpectedly, even if it doesn't look like coffee or smell like coffee but it looks good, drink it. Take action, open the door, be aware that you asked for the answer and that might be the answer you were looking for.

My story chapter 47 part 3... I was going to be a rock star. Actually I was going to be a rap star. I had a group and we made music. We sold music and performed at shows. We even had girls following us and doing things that girls are not supposed to do at that age. We were not making any money, we were only local but I was going to be a rock star. I kept recording music, and doing shows for 6 years. I worked at different jobs and had money. A few opportunities popped up for us to go further in the industry, some of the people we were working with had gotten music contracts but it was never really a serious thing for us. I remember when we opened a show for a one hit wonder group at the time, they were very popular and it was a great moment for us. After the show we met the manager of the group and they were interested in doing something with us. The group was from Detroit, which was 2 hours away from where we lived, however, we didn't jump in the car, go there and meet with them, we didn't send them new music, we didn't follow them to some of their other shows; we just waited for them to make all the effort. We were not focused on being successful, we were distracted by the girls, making music and didn't put enough effort into selling and promoting the music. We had talent and could have made a mark on the industry but we didn't drink the coffee. We didn't get serious about what we had, we didn't make the sacrifices needed to really succeed in the industry. We were too busy being locally famous, we expected someone else to do the work for us.

This is what I mean when I say you have to drink the coffee. As time went on and the music game changed, we quickly became old news and had to find other things to do. Most of us moved on from music as a career completely, others became full–time club Deejays and local music producers, but none of us ever hit that type of popularity again. We had our chance, we drew the opportunity to us but we didn't jump on it when the chance was there.

You have to be alert and know what you are trying to draw to you. Know what you are asking for and look for a sign. Keep focused on it and be ready to learn. Wake up and smell the coffee and when you smell it, drink it.

This chapter was all about growing your awareness not only for what you want, but for what you ask for. The universe wants to deliver to you what you ask for but it can only do this in a few ways. The main way and the one we focus on is opportunity. Sometimes the opportunity will appear as luck or circumstance. Being in the right place at the right time. This is not the case. It is an answer to a request you sent out. It has come to you in the form of an opportunity as a way for you to achieve that which you are focused on. The key is to be able to recognize the opportunity.

For this exercise I want you to look at the list you wrote from the previous chapter of things and experiences you would like to have. I want you to choose three things from the list. One major one and two minor ones. Sitting in a chair in an upright position with your eyes closed. I want you to relax and concentrate on those three things.

Start to see the detail in the experience and feeling of achieving these things. See who is there, the sounds around you, the scents in the air, how you feel. Take slow deep breaths in through your nose, let the air fill your lungs and tighten your stomach muscles, holding it for a second, then breathing out slowly through your mouth. Repeat this breathing pattern throughout the exercise as you focus on the three things. Do this each day for seven days.

After the seven days you will become more aware of the hidden opportunities that surround you, you will start to see how they relate to the three things on your list. You will start to see the path from where you are now and where you want to be.

This is the beginning of your visualization. In another chapter we will work on adding more detail to the vision.

Pamela will now show you how to use the greatest gift you already possess, and make it work for you in the most positive way.

SIX

Gratitude

*"At times our own light goes out and is rekindled by a spark
from another person. Each one of us has cause to think with
deep gratitude of those who have lighted the flame within us."*
*Albert Schweitzer (1875-1965) Nobel Peace Prize
Winning Medical Missionary and Philosopher*

Giving thanks is immeasurable in the process of gaining any
value to your life because it is a Universal Law. It is what the
law requires for you to move forward to the monetary things,
relationships and situations you want out of life. None of
these have staying power without gratitude, it is enormous.
All of the great, Spiritual teachers speak immensely on this
subject.

Have you done something really nice for someone and
not receive the appreciation from the person you felt you
deserved? I think we've all been down this road at some time
or another. You may have thought, at the time, *"Why did I
bother? That person doesn't deserve what I did for them."* Or it
may have been something you gave to them that cost more
than you could afford and they did not seem to appreciate

the value of the gift the way you would have done. Just revisiting these particular times gives validation as to how important appreciation and gratitude are to us. This is how the Law of Attraction works also. If we are not appreciative and show gratitude for what life gives to us then those wonderful gifts will not continue to show up in our lives.

There is a law of gratitude and it goes like this...when you are grateful and feel it and say thank you in your thoughts then you draw positive energy to you which draws positive circumstances and conditions also. This isn't something you have to wait for, it happens immediately and the more you gives thanks with true feelings, the more you draw this energy to you, and the more agreeable and pleasant things enter your life.

The next step is to always be aware of these generous gifts life gives to you. It is easy to take them for granted without being grateful, remember the friend that you thought unappreciative? Well without gratitude all of these enjoyable gifts will stop.

Our problem is there is so much negativity around us we allow ourselves to be drawn into it, and in no time we have slipped back into our old ways. If we are not guarding our thoughts then we won't even see the gifts we are given. So we have to be sure we are alert and aware constantly.

My life was in a bit of a turmoil around 12 years ago, I felt I was between a rock and a hard place; I had been made redundant from a job I had occupied for eighteen years; I was at a loss. My husband was the president of our local cricket club. He was busy running it, which was taking most of his time. He went soon after his evening meal, to the club, and was gone all weekend. When I complained about this, his answer was, I should come to the club and hang out with him there. It was mostly men and I wasn't interested in cricket. I didn't see this as a solution at all, therefore I complained to him constantly, I complained to my friends, in my thoughts and I felt neglected and alone. He was having a good time, he enjoyed running the club, being in charge and he couldn't see the problem. He had done this for eight years. However, the first few years he hadn't been sinking as much time as he eventually did. I couldn't see how we could move forward. It seemed to me like our marriage was deteriorating. I knew I couldn't force him to leave the club, I knew this had to be his decision. If it weren't, he would not be happy and he would possibly resent it.

I then read a book that talked about using gratitude and how powerful it was. I realized I was giving powerful energy in a negative way so this was what I was receiving back. I started to think about the fortunate things that were still a part of our lives together, how he worked so hard each day of the week and never complained about going to his job. How he was generous towards me and didn't worry about my staying home. The thoughts started to mount up as to why I should be grateful towards him. I gave complete gratitude in my heart, and let the negative thoughts go, then it happened!

First of all I found a very good job, one I had wanted. This filled my time, giving me back my credibility. A few months later my husband came home from the club one day and out of the blue, said he'd had enough of the club and he was giving it up. He felt the guys were unappreciative, saying he had done his bit and was going to retire as the president. I was really shocked. It was his idea and he has never regretted his decision. Subsequently, things have been going wonderfully ever since. Regardless, I still always give gratitude for him and all of what we have together.

When we are grateful, the Law of Attraction mirrors it back to us. Sometimes looking back on early memories help us to understand there have been many things we should have been more grateful for, then we think about our present situation and if you feel you don't have much to be grateful for now, then be thankful for your health, or your hearing and sight, that you have energy or that you can breathe with healthy lungs.

We have many things, people and situations to be grateful for. This is one situation that came to my mind. I use to drive on the highway quite a bit for my job. Quite often I would be upset with the massive trucks (lorries) that were also on the highway. They always seemed so intimidating, and I would be annoyed at the way they seemed to dominate the lanes. But now I know better and feel grateful to them as I pass them by. If it weren't for truck drivers, we wouldn't have our food being imported from all those wonderful places they go to and bring back to our stores. We couldn't just go to a store and buy our furniture or our computers or our hair and skin products or our clothes and shoes or our cars or our... well you get the picture. Truck drivers drive in all sorts of weather at all times of the day and night, all year long through all kinds of conditions. I realized we should be totally praising our truck drivers so I make sure I always do these days. Now as I pass them I give a silent *Thank You*, from my heart. And then there are our firefighters, our police force and our ambulance drivers who keep us safe and risk their lives to do so. Just think about the guys that are constantly fixing our roads. Have you been to a country that doesn't have the monetary funds to fix their roads? The roads become very dangerous. It is frightening to drive on them at times. And how about our precious water? There are so many countries that don't have running water. Water is essential to our living. Besides our personal hygiene and sanitation it is a vital commodity for our survival. So we have to thank our city council and government for our water. And then there are our fishermen who risk their lives for our wonderful fish meals, and what about our construction workers who scale the heights of narrow beams and risk their lives to build wonderful buildings and our high-rise apartments. We must always be grateful for our farmers who get up when we are sleeping and battle the weather for our natural, fresh food, as they drive heavy, dangerous equipment. We must give praise and thanks to all of these people that are in our lives each day behind the scenes. There is a long list of these people that are working for our benefit and it goes on... So you see, besides all of the personal reasons to be grateful, there are thousands of other reasons and people we should be totally thankful for.

The Law of Gratitude also helps you to eliminate the negative situations in your life, but you have to feel the gratitude you give. If you say it without meaning, *'Ok, thanks!'* and without much feeling, then it doesn't work. This Universe is a feeling Universe, and your feeling of great appreciation magnetizes more good and great things to you. So give thanks to the small things that happen in your day and you will attract more good things.

Negative thinking is very draining and makes you feel heavy, bringing you to a low point. This is because you are drawing the negativity to you and actually away from the person or situation you are upset with. The person or situation does not reap that negativity, only you do. And it drains you. Essentially it is a misuse of extremely good energy. When I understood this and the power of gratitude I began to think differently, I reminded myself often that it is me who will suffer from harsh thoughts of someone else.

I started to change my view of things and life. I'm no saint, but I did start to think more about me and realized my anger and jealousy can only hurt me, not the other person. Once I started to replace those thoughts with appreciation of the good things in my life those negative situations started to fall away. Of course I still have negative situations—that is life trying to show me lessons I need to learn; and I still feel hurt or disappointed at times but nothing compared to how I used to feel. *I now know I have the power to control those negative thoughts and I no longer give those thoughts power over me.*

We do receive a great deal more than we give in life although we don't really think of life this way. We take so much for granted. Look for the blessings in your life, they are there. If we want to turn any situation around we must be appreciative of the good we have in our lives.

All of the enlightened minds of this world past and present, have used gratitude constantly. *Albert Einstein* was a great scientist but he told us the secret to his success was gratitude.

Oprah Winfrey has often asked guests on her show, *"What do you know for sure?"* At one time I thought this to be a difficult question but this is what I know for sure: *We are all unique and magical human beings. We all have our own talents and we all have our own place in this world. We are all divinely guided and protected and all of us can make a difference in this world and in our own lives if we believe.*

Look for the gifts in everything, even in the negative situations, they are there. And if you want to change your life quickly to bring more joy, put your energy into gratitude, you will certainly see a difference in your life. This, I know for sure.

So remember to count your blessings and to say 'Thank You,' for all that is good in your life.

Here is your exercise for this chapter. You are going to start a Gratitude Journal. Each night as part of your nightly routine. You are to enter 10 things you should be grateful for. Write 'Thank You,' three times next to each one, and feel really appreciative. You will see how positive energy starts to seep into the deeper parts of you. This small act will be the start of a great change in your life.

Back to W.T....

SEVEN

How Does a Sports Team go from Worst to First?

"That a man can change himself, improve himself, re-create himself, control his environment, and master his own destiny is the conclusion of every mind who is wide-awake to the power of right thought in constructive action."
Christian D. Larson (1874-1954) Your
Forces and How to Use Them.

I guess the first thing they need to do is to recognize they suck. They need to do an assessment of what is working and what is not. They need to see why it is they are not able to compete at the level they expected to. Once this is done, they need to figure out where they want to go. Sports are a great way to learn how to manage your life and your business. All the things a sports team goes through are the same things you go through in your life and in your business. You can learn from their successes and failures.

My story Chapter 17 part 162... I remember when I was running production I would watch NFL football. I would study how Belichick would handle injuries, how Dungy would handle a loss, how Cower would manage a close game. When people would ask me who my favorite team was I would tell them, *"I follow the coaches as much as I follow the teams."* I would look at my production areas as parts of a football team. In football you have offense, defense special teams, players that only play one position and other players that can play many positions. You also have players that only come in for certain situations or packages. I identified members of my staff to see who would be good for cross training, so when holiday times came around, I wasn't scrambling or building, 'just in case' stock. Football taught me how to plan ahead. When a player gets injured, even if it is the quarterback, the good coach already has a plan in place. They practice with back up players just in case. In production I adapted the same concept with cross training. I could move my staff around like it was a chess game. I would amaze my bosses by meeting deadlines often without overtime because as I adapted the things I was learning from football, I was becoming a more efficient manager. Before I ever knew the benefits of focus and controlling thoughts I was already using some of the principles.

So what does a sports team do to change?

Like us, they have to do things differently. They have to see things through new eyes. They have to think differently to bring new results. Here comes my favorite word again, they have to focus on the end result. Focus, focus, focus. So how do you retrain your brain to focus on the end result? You need to make a written plan, read the plan, believe in the plan and follow the plan. You have to see the end result in your mind first, then write down what it looks like, write down what the end result looks like, not how you get there, just the end result.

I did this for how I wanted my life to look like. I wrote the type of house that I wanted to live in, the type of car I wanted to drive, the position I wanted to hold at a job, how my finances would look, how my relationship will be, I wrote all of these things as if they had already happened. I added it to my routine; I tried to focus on it every day. I tried to keep this picture on my mind every day. What I found was, it was too large of a picture to focus on all at once. I needed to focus on one part of the picture at a time, achieve that part and then focus on the next part. I realized a sports team doesn't fix everything at once. They fix the defense first and then the offense, or they change the coach and see how that works. They might change the General Manager, but they never change the whole team in one move. Once I started to tackle it in this way, I could see how my focus was changing the outcome, changing the now. I could measure it. What you need to do is identify all the things you would like to change, then determine in what order you would like to change them. Sometimes the little things are first to build up your momentum for change. The thing I focused on first was money. We all like more money no matter how much you have! I would write how I was grateful for the money in my life, grateful for the money I was receiving, and grateful for the money that was on its way to me. Money started to flow and come easily to me. It was there when I needed it and I started to believe in the positive materials which I'd begun reading. I wanted to get a better handle on this so I could improve the other things on my list.

What I had to understand is, to know is not success. Success is brought by action. Action is amplified and secured in success by discipline. Discipline is practice, dedication and routine. Routine becomes habit and habit becomes natural and natural is subconscious. Discipline regulates and monitors your success and enables you to focus on your goals. This is exactly what a sports team does. They have one common goal they are all working toward, winning the championship.

If your business doesn't have this goal then you just have a group of people working for you to do business. They do not know what their real goal is; they are not inspired to be great. Greatness is what we are all here for. To truly be great at what you do, to inspire others to be great too. You can do this in your personal life. You can set the goals you want and train your brain to focus on them. This is a pursuit you must have to control the outcome. Leave nothing to chance, see your future in your mind before it happens and think it into the now.

You need to create a routine like an athlete sticks to a training routine. Week after week they train and improve sometimes in very small increments until the day they see their skills are at the level they aspire to be. This is the way we achieve our goals and guarantee our success. This is the discipline that we pursue.

There are very few things in life that you are good at the first time you try. Learning is a journey and success is earned, not given.

A sports team exists to win. Winning brings income, profit and longevity. An athlete competes to win. Winning brings a career, income, profit and longevity. We exist to win at what we do. Winning brings a career, income, profit and stability.

The more successful I became as a production manager, the more money I made in salary and bonuses. I was able to gain confidence in my decisions, knowing the outcome before it happened. The crazy thing is that I had not learned about the power of focused thought yet. This was a natural way for me so when I learned the power of focused thought the results became amazing. When I started to learn how to use this tool to make my life greater I saw an increase in sales. I started to focus on the accounts I wanted to win. I started to focus and plan in my mind getting orders from these accounts. I could see having the order and processing it before I even bid on the account. The more I focused on getting the account the less I panicked when the opportunity came to bid on the order.

I started to feel like I already had the order and didn't worry about which competitors were chasing the order. Of course, I still did my due diligence and understood who was bidding and tried to find out their price point, but there was not a feeling of nervousness that I might not get the order. What I found was I had a very large increase in closing my quotes. I started to really believe I would get the order. I made a list of the accounts that I wanted to win for the calendar year and started to track what date I secured the order. The list was starting to get crossed off after two-months and began to fuel my confidence in the process.

One of the strengths that athletes have is a tool called visualization. It has been touched on in many books and documentaries. I watched it in the video called 'The Secret,' and it was all about seeing yourself competing in the event before you actually do it.

At first I thought this was crazy, these guys are full of it, and then I realized that trying this would not harm me. It would not hurt me, it is free to do, and if it doesn't work I haven't lost anything. More importantly, if I didn't try it and some of my competitors were, I would be at a disadvantage. In life and in business you should always look for the advantage. Sometimes it means working with people that you would not be friends with outside of work. Sometimes it means taking a risk that others are afraid to take, although we now know all of our risks are calculated and rehearsed in our minds first.

Sometimes it means learning something new, thinking outside the box, going left when everyone else is going right. Sometimes it just means doing something first before everyone else catches on.

There is always someone that can do what you do. There are always people learning new things and skills. Sports teams that go from worst to first have a vision and a plan. They know where they want to end up. They have a goal and they adapt to gain the advantage over the other teams. They take advantage of all opportunities available. They invest in development and improvement. They recruit talent. They read, and seek mentors and advisors. They align with the talent necessary to reach the goal. They focus and stay focused until they achieve the goal. This is the dedication we need to achieve our goals in business and in our personal lives. This is why we create a routine and stick to it day after day. This is why we invest time and energy into our personal development. This is how we come in first.

For this exercise I want you to pick a big goal from your list. You need to think about this big goal and really focus on what it would be like to achieve it or experience it. Get in touch with the feelings of having it. Start to tell yourself you will have it. Write down what it is again on a new piece of paper in detail but at the end of the description add a date. This is the date that you will achieve this goal. Don't make the date too short. Give yourself time to draw the opportunity to you. The stronger you get at manifesting the faster you will be able to achieve your goals. Using the visualization technique from before, sit in a chair again and focus on experiencing this goal each night for 21 days. Read your description each day and visualize the event until it seems more like a memory you've already experienced, than a goal you are reaching for.

In the next chapter Pamela will give you techniques throughout the chapter to help enhance your visualization.

EIGHT

Think Wealth

"Man's right to life means his right to have the free and unrestricted use of all the things which may be necessary to his fullest mental, spiritual and physical unfoldment; or, in other words, his right to be rich."
Wallace D. Wattles (1860-1911) The Science of Getting Rich.

Money is power no matter how you look at it. It gives you a voice in this world. Without money your voice in this world is feeble, sometimes even unheard. Without money you can barely help yourself let alone anyone else. Money is important, don't let us be mislead to believe that it is not.

See Money in a New Light

The majority of us have been told that riches are for those already rich and if we are struggling it is the way it is supposed to be. This came from affluent beings of our world, centuries gone by, who told those of us who were not fortunate enough to be born into wealth, we had to live the life that providence allotted us. Which meant there was no other way for us, if we were born poor that was our lot in life, our fate, and we should be grateful for anything that we got out of our struggles. The preachers told us, at that time, that it was God's will that we should be poor and stay poor.

This was a way to 'keep us all in our places.' What was even more sorrowful is, our ancestors believed it and worse than that, these messages are deep within our psyche today. We have been given to understand that money is something we can have for a short while, for instance our paychecks, and it is not supposed to stay with us because it is not our right to keep money. With these negative thought processes parading around our minds and feeding every part of us, it isn't a great surprise we are not wealthy and don't really believe it is possible that we ever will be.

Our great grandparents accepted this message and thrust it onto our grandparents, they in turn imparted this to our parents and they to us. Without our awareness we in turn transmit this same message to our children, and so it goes.

Flaws and defects of ourselves originate from our attachments to these beliefs. But the truth is we have as much right to be living a rich and abundant life as any millionaire or billionaire living today have. We just have to free ourselves from this attachment of limitation and negativity by thinking abundance and all that abundance entails. When we understand this we find it is the fuel that will enable us to master our own financial security.

Shifting our Focus

This is what happened to me and some fellow workers which convinced me of how powerful our thoughts really are. I had just stumbled upon the book and film, *'The Secret,'* and found it fascinating, so I bought copies for my three sons, gave one to each of them, and then I bought more for some relatives and friends, who I thought it may help. I also bought the same book and film for some of my co-workers. At work, around four of us started to try and think positive thoughts and not complain. We really became quite motivated with all of this new way of thinking. Gratitude is major in all of this so we all became grateful and tried to look at life and our job very differently.

We were a little department of professionals and had not been feeling validation for the work we were doing. Prior to our change of thought and attitude, we complained miserably about this. A few months earlier we had taken our complaints to the union and had been told because we were under the umbrella of, 'casual staff,' we really didn't have many rights at all. Then unbeknown to me and my co-workers, a grievance went forward from two full time members of staff. The grievance was about working conditions and hours, which had nothing to do with us. It went to arbitration. Our union representative explained later to me that the arbitrator questioned not only the conditions of the two employees that had grieved, but also asked about the casual staff and our working conditions. We were somehow brought into the negotiations by the arbitrator. The two staff who had put in the grievance not only got what they wanted but we were given a large pay raise! We had no idea about this and you can imagine the surprise when we were told. This was another way of proof to me that this Universe stuff works. I immediately realized the power of what we can do by thinking positively. It is amazing.

To Make a U-Turn

Regardless, money is the most strenuous situation to get our thoughts around. I have found this very difficult. These negative messages of poverty repeat themselves far too often to us. All the knowledge we have been fed throughout our life has made up our paradigm of assumptions, concepts, values, and practices that constitutes our way of viewing our financial reality. It is this paradigm of thoughts that keep us where we are today. Our job is to make a U-turn and break free from these old views that have been our past thinking. We have to step outside of this box and create a new pattern of understanding. If we don't, we will not change our way financially because those ideas and beliefs are what have been holding us back until now. These beliefs repeatedly tell us we have no right to have money and be wealthy, so deep within our psyche we are confined in that padlock of thought. We are literally in a jail and cannot move forward without breaking free from those thoughts of limitation.

It is essential that we change these messages or they will always be upfront on the center stage of our lives. Many of today's teachers have struggled with this same issue. As tyrannically as our money situation may appear we can get our thoughts around this and we can come to the understanding that we have as much right to be rich as anyone on this earth has.

As a result of my discovery of how our thoughts really do predict our lives and the way to become rich, I realized that there was a certain formula that needs to be in place to accomplish this. Gratitude is number one, we have to be grateful on a daily basis, or as much as we can be.

All of this starts with our change of attitude which comes with our change of thoughts. If our attitude is of thanks and we look at our cup being half full instead of being half empty, this is the beginning of the change to our present situation. Taking things for granted is a major course of negativity. If we are only grateful for our jobs when we hear of cutbacks or layoffs then we are not being truly grateful that we have a job. And we have to be grateful for the money we have had throughout our lives. Think of your past and who provided the food and all that was necessary to keep you alive. Were you grateful for them? Are you still giving thanks for those who provided for you? We have to be grateful to whoever provided these things for us. Do you see? We have to remember how we came to be where we are today. We have to give gratitude for the job we have now while we have one, not just when we think we may lose it. Consequently, we have to be grateful for the money we have now and as a result we will accumulate more. This is also how we open the door to receive what we desire in life. Our healthy attitude is the way it starts and our thoughts give us access to open that door.

This next procedure is one of the hardest ones to follow. Feeling good about money is also key, but this is also the hardest barrier we have to somehow get over. When we feel negativity and give feelings of lack and limitation, this is what we expect deep down in our psyche and the Law of Attraction grants us what we expect all of the time. Our feelings actually vibrate the money to us. Here is an idea to get around this, the next time you receive any money, or your paycheck, try not to think of the bills that will come out of it when you receive it. Try and feel what you would feel if you were given it and it were all yours without anything having to be paid from it. Try and harness those feelings and keep them because you can worry all day about the bills you have to pay but they will still be there. Regardless, if you replace your anxiety about not having enough money, and begin to feel good about money, the money situation will turn around. This is the way you start to change the negative feeling you have about money. Without making a substitute of negative feelings for positive feelings about money, your money situation will stay the same and you won't be on the frequency of receiving money.

When my husband and I had first bought our house my husband persuaded me to save our money and pay off the mortgage as soon as we could. We both worked and although we had good paying jobs we had three sons to rear. I didn't want to struggle to do this but I went along with the thought of how affluent we would be when we became mortgage free. Our mortgage was fully paid by the time I was 35. My husband and I had worked hard and had gone without to pay it so early. At that time we saved all the extra money we could. All I could think about was the freedom of not having a mortgage. I thought about all the money we would have, and how we could afford to buy so much more when the mortgage was finally paid!

Unfortunately when we paid off the mortgage, our ideal situation of being mortgage free didn't happen. Although me and my husband didn't have to pay a mortgage, we did not see a difference in our bank account and the money still seemed to slip away.

We could not understand this and we both complained constantly about not having extra money. This went on for years until I came across the knowledge of the Law of Attraction and began to understand how it worked. As soon as I brought gratitude to the money that we received, instantly it started to grow. My husband repeated the words, *"I don't get this, how come we now have more money in the bank?"* He didn't really believe in the Law of Attraction and so I repeated back, *"It's from the Universe!"* He would laugh and shake his head but he couldn't deny that something phenomenal was at play.

We are extremely happy and grateful that we have paid our mortgage and for the first time in years we have started to see the results of that freedom.

We had been repelling the extra money that should have been ours by constantly complaining we didn't have extra money. It took us to be grateful and appreciate what we had accomplished before we could break the attachment of lack that we had lived with for so long and be on the frequency of accepting this extra money.

I came to realize through this lesson that while I was saving to pay the mortgage off I was excited to watch the money grow in our bank account, and I could easily focus on what I wanted in life. Nevertheless, when it was actually paid, those old reminders that lay dormant suddenly awoke in my subconscious, and I worried that this extra money would seep through our fingers, and it did! Once I changed my thoughts back to what I really wanted, then again, I was able to make that U-turn.

This was the very first occurrence in my life, with this Natural Law. It gave this belief validation and these magnificent experiences have been happening ever since.

If you don't believe you will have money, then it will not turn up for you. You have to give the feeling of love for anything you want in life including money to break that old attachment of lack and not having money. People that are rich, love money. They think of money all of the time in a positive way. They expect to get it and they do get it. If we don't expect to get it then our wish is granted. Our real work is convincing ourselves of the fact that we are as worthy as anyone else to have money. We must think with gratitude of the joys that money can bring into our lives and appreciate the money we have been able to receive whether in monetary or in material things. Whether little or a lot, appreciation for what we've had and what we have—accumulates to more in our future.

Show Your Appreciation

When I first came to grasp this idea of appreciating money in my past, I wrote a list of all that I had received while a kid. It was very emotional because I suddenly had an epiphany of the extent of what my late father had done for me. When I revisited my past I came to realize how much my dad had worked hard for us all, and that he didn't miss a day away from his job when me and my sisters and brother were kids. It hit me like a ton of bricks that although my parents had to struggle to rear all five of us we did not go without. We always had food on the table, a roof over our heads and clothes on our backs. Despite these facts I had taken it for granted up until that exercise and I felt dreadful I had never really thanked him for his wonderful care of me all of those years I was growing up when he was alive. Just the same, my parents were loving and kind and we were brought up to demonstrate our emotions with hugs and kisses to each other, so I do know he had died knowing how much I loved him and I let myself off the hook of condemnation. You see it is very important that we address our past history, with gratitude, for the money we've had, to bring us into the frequency of accepting what is ours to receive.

Always look upon money with gratitude and without exception, keep that thought alive.

We have to reinvent our feelings about money. We have to celebrate it, if we do we are promised more from a loving universe. This is what all of the modern day teachers say, and believe me, they are all millionaires. What I have come to know for sure is, it really is all about what we expect from life. If we don't expect much, then what we harvest is meager also. We have to get on the receiving end of money and wealth before we can inherit what is rightfully ours.

You have to ignore your current situation as hard as that may be, but if you think with gratitude for having what little you have then you will receive more. This is how you attract money to you. There are trillions of ways money can come to you through the Law of Attraction because this is a Natural Law so there are no limitations if you believe.

However, be on guard and take caution, we should always keep in mind that money is the medium of exchange for happiness and so the things you want with money have to be in harmony with this world—with other people. We cannot profit from their hardship, we cannot use extortion in any degree. In other words we cannot benefit by coercing people to buy invaluable products or experiences to any extent. This is a Universal Law. If we do not comply with this law we will experience lack or sorrow in the degree that we have given it to others.

Also we have to stay clear of competition, our abundance must flow from the fountain of creativity not from competition. We do not have to compete for anything in this world because the Universe gives everyone their own. You and everyone else living have been given wonderful talents which will produce your ideal life. This means that you do not have to fight and scramble for something someone else may also want or have, there is enough for all.

Thoughts lead us to imagination, by using images in your mind of the life you would want to be living, therefore seeing it as reality now, you must believe. When you are on the same frequency the Law of Attraction takes up this picture and works to change from where you are now to where you want to be. Visualization is what bridges the gap and brings you to the life of your desire. This was a very difficult part of this law for me. At first it seemed to me to be quite ludicrous. I couldn't get myself on this frequency at all. It took a lot of reading and realizing that all the teachers and avatars talk about the same thing. What you convince yourself is real—becomes your reality.

This means you have to really use your imagination and feelings, stick to the idea of what you would like to create in your world and keep with it. Think about it ceaselessly and it will appear as your reality. This is the way we overcome those old messages of lack. This is the way it is done.

The Law of Attraction gives to you what you give out. You magnetize and receive the circumstances of money you have placed. This is your investment in yourself. The keys to attracting all of the abundance you desire is: Gratitude, Visualization, Feelings, Acceptance, Belief, and to Receive.

So think large. Visualize the ultimate life that you wish for and see what happens.

In the next chapter W.T will explore money and expectations, and how to apply it to your life right now.

NINE

Does your bank statement make you happy or sad?

"If one advances confidently in the direction of his dreams, and endeavors to live the life which he has imagined, he will meet with success unexpected."
Henry David Thoreau (1817-1862)

Money is the hardest thing to learn how to manage. I have found the more you make, only results in nicer things and a larger debt than when you were making less money. It doesn't mean you have more security; in fact you really have less security because you are a bigger burden to your employer, and, it is harder to manage your debt if something changes in your financial life. As I struggled to stay ahead of my debt through the company going bankrupt I was working for, and through making less money as I brought the company back to life, I never stopped to ask the question: *'Does your bank statement make you happy or sad?'*

Now I have always had a good relationship with money. It has come easily to me. I have always felt I was lucky to constantly find myself in positions that pay well and allow me to build up my cash position, but I never really thought about my financial statement until I was making less money and starting to see my debt build up to a scary level. The truth is, when you are comfortable you believe you will always be comfortable and you think the money will always be there, that is until you get an eye opener.

The reason the company went bankrupt was not because we were not working hard enough. It wasn't because we didn't have lots of orders to fill. It wasn't because the bosses were greedy. It was a mismanagement of funds, plus an over expansion of the company that was not sustainable if there were any shift in the economy. The economy started to tank, triggering a domino effect that led to an overvalued inventory. The bank doesn't like it when you take loans against your inventory then find out the inventory is not worth what the loan is. Now I am not sure who was ultimately responsible for balancing these numbers. I am not sure how the inventory became inflated in value. What I do know is this: The bank called in the loan and the company came to a stop mid production. This was the first time I realized no matter how careful I am with my money, I am not in control of my financial well-being. I am not in control of my quality of life or my standard of living. So who is in control of my financial statement, quality of life and standard of living? Who is in control of yours? How can you get control of all of the above?

The first thing to realize is you can control your future but it will take planning and focus. You can't count on your boss to look after you. You're selling him your services and that is great but at the end of the day he has to look after his business, which may or may not include you as part of the survival plan. Your job is to find ways to protect yourself from this situation.

You will need to learn a few key techniques to help increase your chances of financial independence

1. Money is an attitude. You must believe that money comes easily to you and you have an abundance of money. You have to be more than happy to pay your bills. You have to stop worrying about not having enough money and start focusing on what you can do to have more money. Instead of saying *"I can't afford that,"* you need to say, *"What can I do to afford that?"*

We live in a society that sees the rich as being very lucky, privileged, or lazy, born into prosperity, and the rest of the people are just accepting this is how it is and that they cannot do what the rich have done. The reality is the rich are not lucky, they are not privileged and they may not even be very smart with their money. What they do that others do not do, is look at something and ask, *"What do I need to do to be able to afford that?"*

2. To be happy about your financial statement you will need to take charge of your money, like they said at a *'Rich Dad'* seminar I went to; *"You have to give your money a job."* Your mind is your best asset, don't waste it on petty things. You need to focus on how you want your financial statement to look. Figure out what you need to do to generate more

money. The solution is different for everyone. Find out what things you are good at, what your talents are, and remember you have many talents. See if any of those talents can be used to bring more money into your life. Keep your mind open to new opportunities.

Network with people and see if there is anyone around that might want to work with you or partner with you. The mind is a very powerful tool that you have at your disposal; learn to use your mind to bring opportunities to you.

My story Chapter 8 part 22... When I decided to move on from my job and I really let go of the job, I felt a weight lifting off of me and I felt it was now okay to move on and look at other ventures. I had been at the job in some position or another for 14 years. I grew up during my time there, 3 of my 4 kids were born while holding that job. The process to get me to the point of no longer caring about what is good for the company was a long and painful one. I struggled with this decision for more than a year, always talking myself out of it and choosing to stay and help the company. As I gained the confidence in my abilities and recognized the transferable value that I possessed, it became easy for me to start to look for the next great job. I kept thinking about being happy in a new job and working with new people. I wasn't scared at all, instead I felt powerful. There was nothing that could stop me, nothing holding me back. I could see my future as a bright and wonderful one.

I met a guy in Wal-Mart as I was looking for a booster seat for my son. He was looking for one too but he was also looking for salespeople to help boost his business. I started getting calls for interviews. I was turning down jobs weekly knowing there were better offers around the corner. I wasn't nervous that I wouldn't get a better opportunity than the one I just turned down. I knew without a doubt I would find what I was looking for. I not only attracted an offer that was so great my old job couldn't match it, but I also attracted people I had worked with before, who could help me start in a key position in the new company. At that point in my life I knew I was in control of my financial future because no matter what happened I knew I could attract another job and I would always have money. This is a real power you can develop. It is a mental strength. The question is how did I learn to develop this power?

3. Everything starts with an idea or a need. If you are already happy with your cash position that is great, protect it and grow it. If you are sad with your cash position now is the time to change it. There is nothing standing in your way. Your job is to simply think about it and make a plan.

My story Chapter whatever... The truth is, my journey didn't start at the moment I decided the job was no longer good for my financial future. The journey really started a year and a half before. It was near the end of November. I realized that I couldn't afford to give my kids much for Christmas. I couldn't afford to give my relatives much for Christmas either. I felt so bad and ashamed, not because it is important to give people things but I'd felt like I let myself down by accepting the situation, not doing anything to change the situation. I never looked at what I could do to change my financial statement. In January of the following year, my wife begged me to attend a '*Rich Dad*' Seminar. She had been to the intro one (the free one) and bought tickets to the 3-day seminar. This was taking place at the beginning of the NFL play offs. It was wild card week-end, I'd waited all year for the playoffs, and the Steelers were playing on that Sunday. I didn't want to go but she really wanted me to go with her so I reluctantly agreed. What I heard there I had never heard before. What I learned that week-end changed the way I looked at money. To this day I still use a lot of the information I learned.

Now I didn't follow everything we learned and some of the ideas were not for me, but it was the first step in changing the way I think, in taking ownership of my financial future. There was a need that came about and a realization that started the journey of discovery into motion. The thing about change is, you can accept it or fight it but it will happen with or without you. The only difference is; Are you going to control change or is change going to control you? David Bowie said, *"I can't change time but time changes me."*

So the Journey was simply this.

How can I become rich?

This one question took me on a path of successes and failures and led me to learn about the power of the mind and the power of planning and visualizing. There is a discipline that must be developed. A routine that must be followed but the key to all success is very simple and free. It is gratitude.

4. You must be grateful for what you already have. You must be grateful for the life you are living right now. You must say it and repeat it often throughout the day. You must feel the joy of what you have, then you must be grateful for what you *will* have. You have to be grateful for your future and believe you future is guaranteed. That it will happen and you have to focus on that future.

Be grateful for everything in your life. All the ups and downs, the successes and failures, all that you have been given and all that you have earned.

This is a must if you want to make your bank statement bring you joy and happiness. This is one of the things the rich who sustain their wealth do. It is also the thing the rich who lose their wealth do not do. What it means is, you have to appreciate your job, your home, your car, your money... This is not easy to do if you don't like any of those things but if you do not do this it is very hard for you to focus on better things. You see your focus will be on what you don't have and what is missing in your life instead of what is waiting for you around the corner.

5. Thinking is a key part of building success.

Nothing exists without first being born in thought.

Before anything can be built or started, some thought has to be put into it, or at minimum the idea has to exist in your mind. This is why I believe your mind is your best asset. You can see in your mind how you want things to be. You can adjust it and plan around problems to create a blueprint for your next move or venture. This is what successful people do. They focus on the end result and work toward the end result. They foresee the problems that may arise and they plan for them. It is only when they lose focus that things start to go out of control. It is when they are too busy to stop and think things through, that things become unpredictable. Your mind can help you to see what is next before you get there.

Isn't this a huge advantage? To be able to map out your career moves in your head first and see how it will look before you jump in?

These are the methods that I used to gain the advantage over the people I worked for and to gain the confidence to take charge of my own financial well-being. I started to be grateful for the money I was making. I was grateful for the opportunities I had at the job. I was grateful for the car I drove and the expense account I had. I was grateful for the customers I had, and the orders I received from each customer. As I did this simple daily task, I discovered I didn't worry about money any longer. I seemed to have more money somehow. I realized even when I spent the money, more was on its way to me so I could feel good about spending it. I came to a realization, a truth; I am the only one that cares about me and my bank statement so why should I count on anyone else to make sure the conditions for my financial freedom are in place? It is up to me to find the tools for success and learn how to use them. I am my own teacher, my own boss, and my own planner. I have the power to think, to focus, to visualize, and to implement.

Successful people make a plan, put it into action, and reap the benefits. Unsuccessful people make excuses. *Do you make plans or excuses?*

What is stopping you from starting something new? What is stopping you from going for it? You need to write down what you want your life to look like. Add as much detail as you can to it. Focus on it every day, believe that it will happen, know you will succeed. Write about your wealth, health, career, happiness, your wants and desires. Think big, have big ideas and keep them on your mind all the time.

When you are focused on big ideas and big goals you will have no time for the small and petty details. The reason people succeed against the odds is because they use their mind and focus to gain the advantage. They *think* their success into existence. Throughout my life I have been able to do the things I wanted to do without knowing this. The problem was the things I wanted to do were small things in retrospect. Become a supervisor, own a nice house, have a nice car, have some money in the bank, be able to buy beer whenever I wanted to, small ideas that I achieved relatively easily. I never knew that my mind and my focus was drawing these things into my life. When I was just a guy on the shop floor, dreaming of becoming the supervisor, it was more of a fantasy than anything else. I kept thinking about it and what I would do differently if I were in charge.

My story Chapter 15 or 16, part 2.5... I was working a part-time job at a warehouse making good money but the job had no benefits and no opportunity to become a fulltime worker. I had some interviews at some factories but most were saying I needed to learn how to weld and drive a forklift, then they would hire me. So I decided to look for a small company that could provide the experience I needed, then I would be able to re-apply at the jobs I really wanted. I found the company that was the perfect fit for my ambitions. I told myself I would work there for one year then leave for the 'real money.' Soon after I started there, I fell in love with the place and the type of work I was doing. It seemed to be what I was meant to do?!? After a short time I became a lead-hand and was in charge of training new guys and helping to problem solve. The company was growing and needed to start an afternoon shift so they moved the supervisor to that shift leaving me to help the plant manager run the day shift.

As we grew it was becoming too big for the plant manager to run with just a lead hand support so they started to look for a supervisor to help him. The guys on the shop floor didn't like the idea of having a new guy in charge so they started pressuring me to apply for the job as they liked working with me. This was a big step for me. I had never really wanted to be a fancy pants. I applied for the position and got it. My boss told me that he was hoping I would apply for it but didn't want to ask me to apply because he wanted it to be something that I wanted, due to the stressful workload that comes with the job. My mind had put the goal into action and opened doors for me to walk through, but the journey didn't stop there. I became the plant manager and did that role successfully for many years. I was happy and making good money but I took it for granted. I believed I would always have this role and make that money. It was endless. Sure I feared if something should happen, because I didn't have all the education that was needed to go with the experience and knowledge for this particular position. Even so, I didn't do enough things to protect myself just in case. This is the mistake so many people are making in their lives, leaving their financial well-being in the hands of others, not appreciating the now and being grateful for what they have accomplished. If you do not have a constant flow of money coming to you from more than one source, if that one source stops, what happens to you?

This is another way successful people are different from everyone else. They give their money a job, to make more money. They invest a portion of their earnings into growth ventures. The rest of us make more money from raises or bonuses and increase our lifestyle. The more we make the more we spend. We haven't really gained anything, we just have nicer things. Successful people buy nicer things with the extra revenue they are making, it's something you might of heard of before, its call profit. This should be a part of everyone's plan. This is what we should be teaching our children. Get a job or start a business but don't live off of everything you make no matter how small your money is. Don't put it in a bank account that pays almost zero % interest. Put your money to work. Look for ways to make your money grow. Work toward not having to rely on your job for all your cash flow. This is basic common sense knowledge. Strangely, this is not the way our brains have been programmed. We think these are things other people can do because they are lucky. This is what you can do with focus and vision, it is never too late to start thinking and acting this way.

To know is not success; success is brought about by action.

You have to write a plan and then put that plan into action. Nothing will come your way from hope. Hope is chance and chance is unpredictable. Take charge of you. Take charge of your bank statement.

Be patient, be dedicated, and don't get discouraged. Stay focused on the goals.

Learning is a journey and success is a goal that is earned not given.

You must have the vision to do the work, the confidence to put it into action and the dedication to see it through to the end. Everyone wants to make more money. Everyone wants to be rich and successful. The issue is, not everyone is willing to challenge the status quo and do something to change their chances of success. Most people are waiting for their boss to magically promote them, or they are waiting for their lotto numbers to land. They are waiting for something to happen. For someone else to take charge for them and they reap the benefits of that person's labor. They are waiting until it is too late to learn and change.

News flash, the people that are not waiting are rich and successful or at least on the road to riches and success. The people that are not waiting are happy with their bank statement.

So I ask you...

Does your bank statement make you happy or sad?

In the next chapter Pamela will shed some light on the benefits and issues of our health.

TEN

Think Health

"A wise man should consider that health is the greatest of human blessings, and learn by how his own thought can derive benefit from his illness."
Hippocrates (460-377 BC)

We all want wealth, I believe this is a fact. Wealth brings us freedom, we cannot deny this. However, we also need our health because without good health we won't really enjoy the fruits that wealth can bring to us. We all know this even those of you who happen to have very good health most of your life. Just the same, many of you have suffered the flu or a virus or a terrible cold at least once. But some of us have had much worse health issues than a virus.

I want to share my story because if you are looking to change your life and become wealthy, which is your right and is in your control to do so, it is advisable to keep your good health, or restore it, for those of you who are suffering ill health.

99

I had been fairly healthy, I had my share of small issues such as a back problem every once in awhile, a virus and so forth, but I had mainly been in quite good health.

Around 2003 I started to have major issues with my joints. First of all it was in my neck and shoulders which became very painful, and then it progressed. I did the usual over the counter painkillers and so forth to no avail. I tried to handle the situation myself, waiting before I went to see my doctor, I believe, in the hopes that whatever was going on would leave again. It didn't.

Helpful Hands

When I finally made the visit to the doctor, my joints were inflamed to the point that I had trouble buttoning buttons, taking screw type lids off of bottles and generally using simple items and gadget devices. He sent me to a specialist who at first thought I had Lupus and talked about steroids, pills and all sorts of treatments that, to be honest, frightened me. I wasn't willing to accept this. I went to the health food store, got books about joint pain and spent hundreds of dollars experimenting with different natural cures. I went to numerous specialists in the natural health field, none of whom could ease the inflammation. Eventually I went to Kathy, she gave wonderful full body reflexology.

Reflexology is a method of massage that relieves nervous tension through the application of finger pressure, especially to the feet. Kathy also used meridian tapping which is releasing pressure from parts of the meridian points of the body, freeing energy. She was wonderfully helpful but couldn't cure me completely. This all went on for about two years, until I finally went back to my doctor, as by now, I was becoming crippled in my hands and legs. He sent me to a hand therapy clinic at a major hospital in another city. They gave me splints for my hands, which didn't help, and told me that my hands would only get worse, not better. Eventually I was sent to a rheumatologist where I was diagnosed with rheumatoid arthritis. At this point I wasn't surprised. By this time, I was aware I had all of the symptoms, since I had eventually given in, and gone to an appointment, after having cancelled two prior appointments. But by now, I was in a shocking state, struggling to walk. The doctor confirmed it was practically in every major joint of my body! She put me on three different pills. I still kept taking the natural pills, especially the one that built up my immune system.

I was fortunate because I had a mom who was positive when it came to health issues and a friend whose own experience comes next. My mom never gave in to bad health and always took any illness as lightly as possible. She had numerous ailments herself and if we asked her how she was feeling she always told us she was fine, she kept strong. And so I inherited her positive thinking throughout my own ordeal.

Since then I have learned the secret of the Law of Attraction. I realize if we think health we become healthy.

I decided to really bring this into my life and each day I thank the Universe for my health. I am now off of all of my pills, my hands are flexible and back to normal, no one would ever know the joints had been crooked. I have no pain and I am very healthy today with no signs of rheumatoid arthritis. I believe that I am healthier than I've been since I was in my teens.

All the books I have read about our thoughts tell us if we want health we must think health, if we want to be rich we have to think abundance, if we want to be happy we should not complain about our lives but be optimistic and think of all the happiness that we can, and it will be ours.

I was diagnosed with a debilitating disease that is supposed to be incurable. At that time I had a lot of stress in my life. I changed my thought processes, gave gratitude for the good health I have, and everything started to improve drastically. I literally proved to myself that this universe really does love us. My health turned around because I believed it would do so. I expected it to do so. Your thoughts and what you believe is what you are telling your brain cells how your health should be.

Our Powerful and Intelligent Cells

Did you know you have a 100 trillion cells in your body and they all have a specific job to do? Did you know these cells all have a guiding principle which is to be directed to work hard and give you life? When you complain of bad health it is as if you have told them to take time off and although they work, they don't work as hard for you.

Did you know all of these powerful brain cells are under your control and listen to your thoughts constantly? You are literally the commander of this immense army inside your body. This astounding army of cells who are ready to work and fight any unwanted forces in your body wait patiently for your command, like an army waiting for the order. Without it, they are often paralyzed, rendered impotent and eventually give up. They believe everything you believe, so if your thoughts are of ill health, their command is, you don't need them to work hard and they lay dormant. This is when your immune system is left to fend for itself. This is why your body will struggle with an illness. They all have their own particular job to do, and they will do it if you expect them to, and believe they will.

A Healing Faith

When I first came to Canada from England I worked with a Scottish woman I found was absolutely empowered with a special kindness. She was old enough to be my mom and I suppose I adopted her as my Canadian mom, because I missed my own mom so much. Anyway, we spent a lot of time together at work and away from the job in those days, I loved to be in her company because she always made me laugh and she was so much fun to be around. Her husband also worked at the same hospital as we did, and was just as nice as she was. They had been together since she was fifteen years of age and still shown complete respect and care for one another.

One day her husband told me she had gone for tests and they had found cancer in her lymph nodes, He said it didn't look very good. I was absolutely devastated. I cried and cried. I was thirty-one-years old at the time and I hadn't a clue about the Law of Attraction, neither did she. Me and my husband went to see her in hospital, and as soon as I set eyes on her, the tears started to roll down my cheeks. She immediately said to my husband, *"I don't want anyone around me that is being weepy. If they want to cry they can cry for themselves but not for me!"* While I wiped vigorously at my eyes with my Kleenex she said again to my husband, *"Can you believe I only went for a checkup and they tell me this. And me of all people that doesn't smoke and doesn't drink, well you wouldn't really have thought that would you?"* She was actually smiling. I couldn't believe her, she was just the same as if someone had told her she had some minor ailment!

When all the tests came back, she was told the cancer had spread through her entire body. She couldn't believe it, as she'd said she didn't have any signs of illness. She was told she only had months to live. She and her husband decided to get a second opinion and went to a hospital in Toronto. The diagnosis was the same. I have no idea how she kept so optimistic through all of it, but she did. They flew out West to see her brother in Alberta, Canada, and then she took her son and daughter and their families to Walt Disney World in the States, and visited her other brother, who lived in Florida. All the time she kept a confident hope that all would be well.

When she went back for a checkup a year later, they said that the tumors were shrinking and reduced. They couldn't understand what was happening. My friend went on with her life and came back to work and until this day the doctors and specialists have no clue as to what happened. I didn't understand it at that time, but now I know her love of life and the fact that she would not give in, kept her strong. She was grateful for her life. Now with my own circumstances it proves to me more than ever, we all do have control over disease, and anything that tries to enter our body. We just have to believe in our own power.

Stress

What is stress? We understand about stress more than ever before and the damage that it does to our body. It can produce ulcers, high blood pressure, heart disease, anxiety and the list goes on. We know it comes from our deeper thoughts.

We know we produce stress from the situations we meet up with through our lives and also how we deal with those situations. But do we know it is those messages we held onto deep within our psyche that are the underlying problem? Stress comes from our environment and circumstances but it is what we do with those messages that cause our anxiety. Stress has caused us to lose our way and also at times lose our lives.

This dangerous disease hurts us because we neglect to see how we can change it around. Our mind dwells on the things that are negative, and we haven't understood, until now, that we can redirect those thoughts to the positive energy fields which draws more positive circumstances to us and eliminates stress.

Thinking positively has brought people to walk across war zones to safety and transform the most nullifying and adverse situations and conditions to bring remarkable changes of joy into their lives.

We haven't realized we have a choice, until now. Our health is our strength and our strength grows through our health, but thought is the director of our health.

Gratitude is also a major key in healing, even when we are at our worst health. It is the fastest way to really begin to experience the full state of health. We have to keep the thought in mind that we are healthy and thank the Universe, God, our Higher Self, whoever we feel is our life force, and give gratitude for every breath we take. This also prevents illness. So you don't have to wait until you are struggling with some sort of illness before you use gratitude, you can start now. I constantly say, *"Thank you all you powerful cells that are keeping me healthy."* I think of them as my little army and feel the gratitude when I say it; I picture them all working hard for me. Obviously they are listening because I have my health back!

Be rich in health, think healthy thoughts, give gratitude and you will definitely see a change. I did!

Music is also a powerful healer, W.T will show you how it works in his life...

E L E V E N

Sometimes you hear Bob Marley in the strangest places

*"One good thing about music, when
it hits you, you feel no pain."*
Bob Marley (1945-1981)

My story ... I was in the men's washroom at a fancy restaurant sitting for a moment as we do from time to time, there was music playing softly on the PA system and suddenly *Bob Marley's "Waiting In Vain"* came on. I thought, 'Man, what a place to hear good music.' It was not the kind of place I would expect to hear Bob Marley and I never thought I would hear it in the restroom! I was on a sales lunch and everything was going well. Bob put me in a great mood and when I came back from the restroom I was more focused and yet more relaxed than before.

Music can change the way you feel and it can also make a moment memorable. It is the soundtrack for your life. It can influence the way you think and it can shape your views and attitude. I grew up hearing *Bob Marley*, I was probably hearing him in the womb. Sometimes when I am watching a movie Bob will be playing in a scene or I will hear Bob for a moment on a T.V show. You never know when you will hear *Bob Marley.*

My story chapter 91 part 5... I was working as a janitor in a hospital for the mentally challenged. They lived there full time, so each area or wing was a living area and housed people of the same level of ability. My area to clean, at that time, was for higher functioning residents. Often I would go there at the start of the shift and see people waking up and starting their day. I would clean the rooms while they were gone for breakfast and clean the washrooms and shower rooms later in the morning. The job was alright but it was not a glory job.

The best thing about the job was the pay check. Each morning was relatively the same, by eleven o'clock the T.V room would have *Bob Barker with the TV game show, 'The Price Is Right'* on, and I would be finished in that area by lunch time and on to the next area for the afternoon cleaning. One morning I arrived and started to get my cart ready, and that's when I heard it: *"jamm'in we jam'in jamm'in out straight from yard."* I was so happy that I left my cart to see what was going on. One of the counsellor's was playing the legends CD in the family room on the big stereo at 7:10 in the morning. I had never heard anyone playing Bob there before. He told me he loves Bob and that Bob made him feel good, just like me. I never really interacted with many of the counsellor's there before that, but this broke the ice and we would chat often after that day.

Bob had a way of bringing people together and breaking down barriers. It is strange, the power that music can have on someone. It is surprising how many people like *Bob Marley's* music.

People from all walks of life know who he is and know some of his music. I have worked with people that didn't like black people and didn't want to know anything about the culture until they went to Jamaica for a vacation. They would come back with an open mind and a thirst for the fun of the Caribbean culture. They would even ask me if they could borrow some of the music or how they could cook some of the food. They always came back more friendly and wanted some *Bob Marley* music so they could keep that feeling of a great vacation for as long as possible.

Music is an important part of my life. It has always accompanied all my big events and has always been there to enhance my mood or change it when necessary. Every BBQ event, every party, every time someone came over, music would be playing and smiles would be abundant. Life is always more fun when you add music to it. Imagine watching a movie or T.V show without music. Imagine going to the fair and not hearing music playing. Imagine going to a festival and not hearing any music. It just wouldn't be as good or as memorable.

My story chapter 5 part 10... I was on a school trip to the Royal Canadian Museum. We were looking at all the exhibits and each floor had different themes. We were in the Chinese exhibit looking at the different dynasties and

I hear *"Three Little Birds"* but it wasn't *Bob Marley* singing, there was no one singing. It was my teacher whistling the tune as he walked through the exhibit. I was shocked! I never thought he would know who *Bob Marley* was, let alone know any of his songs. I asked him if he were whistling *Bob Marley,* as I thought for sure there must be another song that sounds like *"Three Little Birds."*

He laughed and asked me if I was surprised he knew the tune. He told me they listened to a lot of Bob when he was in University. You just never know who is a fan.

Bob can inspire you to keep on movin,' he can inspire you to stir it up, he can inspire you to stand up for your rights. He is love, peace and equality. He is still influencing people long after he was here. I was only 12 when he passed away. I didn't even really know why he was so important or what he meant to the world.

From Rwanda to the Far East, people are singing his tunes. Rock stars love him, country music stars love him, teachers, politicians, and bankers love him. At any given time you can hear his music somewhere. People will always surprise you when it comes to *Bob Marley.*

You never know when you will be reading a book and out of nowhere there could be a chapter about *Bob Marley!!!*

Let's talk about talent, with Pamela, we are all creative people.

T W E L V E

Your Talents and Creativity

"Real power comes from within. All power that anybody can possibly use is within man, only waiting to be brought into visibility by his first recognizing it, and then affirming it as his, working into his consciousness until he becomes one with it."
Charles Haanel, The Master Key System.

This stage is where it can become very confusing or very exciting. As we have mentioned, your creative powers are already within you. You have many talents waiting to be brought to action. These have been given to you for a reason, and this reason is for you to become all you have longed to be. This is where you become the Master Mind of your own life.

No person on this earth needs to envy another person for what they have. None of us need to be jealous, or try to take it from them, or wish them to lose what they have, because all that they have, you can have also, and this ability is produced from your own gifts of creativity. You only have to call it into existence.

Your job is to discover that special ingenuity within you. It is yours alone and you will know when you have discovered it, since it will instantly bring to you an excitement you cannot suppress. This talent is eager to come out. It wants to be a part of your future because it was already conversant with the plan of your life.

No one but you can discern what talent you have. You are the only one that can search this out. Many people have followed their parents dream, or someone else's dream, and have been guided to talents they have initiated through that person's desire and not their own. They may have put major work into this idea that was planted for them and arrived at a wonderful career, but they will not find the satisfaction or the gratification they would have, had it been their own legitimate gift.

We all have desire, but most people's desire is superficial therefore impotent on the account that they, themselves, do not stir the positive energy their desire needs to move forward. It's like stirring the pot with the wrong mixture, if it doesn't have the right ingredients it won't taste good.

Many people already know clearly what their passion is in life, what they want to do and where they want to take it, but as W.T said, they tend to talk themselves out of taking their gifts to the next level. We often think we need large amounts of money to start with, however, this is not the case with the universe. We need to believe in the talent that was given to us and use it with gratitude.

When you are inspired from your inner creativity, act on it. You will know when you have connected with it from the enormous enthusiasm that is within you. It will be all you think about and visualization comes easy to you as this desire grows.

Leave No Room For Doubt

But take heed to this warning, there is a danger that can dampen the most enthused person and that is doubt. This uncertainty will present itself to you. If you give in to it, it will take root, then failure takes its place and your creativity will be crushed. This is where many people go wrong. They become doubtful, and then frustrated with their idea, struggle with it, see faults with it and give up. They have invited negative energy where there was positive energy. They've allowed the doubt to scatter their thoughts and take control. This doubt demands an end to your idea, then you give in to it. I've been there. I think we all have at some point. In fact many of us have been there numerous times.

We have to make a stand against doubt. We have to replace doubt as soon as it enters and safeguard ourselves with positive thoughts. We have to be aware of this assailant entering unauthorized into our creativity. We have to stand strong and steadfast the moment it enters, because it will. Make all of your focus directed to the chosen desire you are now creating. There can only be one channel to this inspired creativity and it cannot be contaminated with fear or doubt. If we concentrate all the power on the desire we have chosen then it will not fail us because the power comes from within. When we turn to doubt we are turning to our external environment which does not have the power to put into creation our desire, and this is where we will fail.

A Call To Action

Once we understand our own power through the Universal Law, we should conclude that there is nothing to fear. This is when we can rightly assume there is one more ingredient we must not overlook, and that is action.

When people have made the connection to their own given talents, they create their life with excitement and it is filled with enthusiasm and fun. The love for this endowment does not feel like work at all. The pleasure that comes from it is amazing.

When you have discovered this creative talent within you, next comes the plan. Plans are action. The Universe will not make a career for you, or create a business from nothing or bring about great changes without you first starting this process. It will not appear in front of your eyes if you don't take the time to put a plan of some sort into action. Bring it to your vision by imagining the plan from the beginning until the end.

You do not have to change your job, or leave it unless you have an offer you cannot refuse. This is where your feelings come into play. When the time is right your intuition will become sharp, your gut feeling will tell you whether you are making good choices or not. You will learn to pay attention to your feelings.

Make your ambition a vital focus in your life. Direct your thoughts to focus on the vision you see in your future. Feel what it would be like if you were living with this desire now. You have to focus on one plan of action and always keep this plan in mind. Whenever you have the time, use it to focus on the idea and the plan of action until it is clear to you.

You have to believe in the vision and have faith that it will come to you without a doubt.

Intend it! Give gratitude. This is your assurance that you will receive your desire when it arrives. Be ready and follow the advice given to you by W.T. Ask yourself the questions he has listed, as they are sound advice to help you in this process. It is also helpful to use positive strong affirmations to reprogram those messages you have lived with for so long. There are many affirmations at the end of this book.

Eventually if you want a career change, if you want to leave your job, you will be led in the right direction, people will enter your life, unexpected events will take place which will lead you to where you need to be.

Challenge Your Imagination

Visualization is also very important in all of this process. You use your imagination in every moment. There are pictures moving through your mind constantly, many pictures will be linked to ordinary circumstances or negative ones if they are not guarded otherwise. Your job from this point on is to give visualization the best pictures you can foresee. Move from the inferior to the extraordinary. Make your future bright, make it big. Imagine yourself with everything you want in life. Bring out the powers you have been given. Do not be afraid of feeling greedy or selfish. Remember that each one of us that moves our energy upwards towards greater things are not only doing it for ourselves; but we are doing it for everyone else, so what is greedy or selfish about that? If you had money and became wealthy, you can help others in a way you haven't been able to do up to this point. Think of the freedom wealth would give to you. Your creativity will bring you to this freedom if you use it wisely and with harmony. It will also bring you more creativity to accomplish all of your dreams and desires.

Meditation is what all the teachers and avatars have used constantly to bring them in connection with this super power. This is a way to bring awareness to positive thinking.

Meditation is a practice to train the mind or induce a mode of consciousness, some meditations include techniques designed to promote relaxation, to clear the mind. There are many different ways to meditate, and so it is best that you find the one which is the most comfortable for you.

When we can quiet ourselves in meditation, we connect to the world within. We bring to light a powerful entity which we feel deep within us. We feel the love and the presence of perfection, and for the first time, we feel our true worth. When we love ourselves fully we extend ourselves to who we really are. We reach a new magnitude of our actual potentialities, we understand they are unlimited. We center our thoughts deep within our being, our true essence, the part within us that holds our value. This part tells us we are love and we deserve all that this loving universe wants to give to us.

Remember whatever we think about deeply and intensely, the subconscious will take up and develop further. Delve into the vast interior realm of your psyche. Interior power comes from the very depth of your subconscious. Direct the subconscious to bring ideas to help you with the plan of action to move your life to the life of your desire. The subconscious will go to work along these lines. You will be impressed by the results and how many ideas that come your way. This is where our great potential lives; this is also our assurance that we can become all that we want to be.

If we give this new presence our deeper attention, answers start to come naturally. We have to think of the idea we want to formulate, then believe that it can be worked out, this way we turn over our thoughts to the profound depth of our subconscious and it then unites with the Universal Infinite Intelligence, God, the Source, the Universe.

Do not become dispirited if this doesn't happen the first time or the first few times you expect your subconscious to go to work for you. You have to really convince yourself of your own worth and values. Remember your subconscious likes repetition. Sometimes it will take awhile for this wonderful power to be reprogrammed. Your job is to believe that it will. Belief given with feeling, are the blueprint of this new process for your subconscious. Once you have faith in what your plan of action is, then your subconscious will take up this conviction because it always believes everything your conscious mind tells it.

In the event that you seem to fail in your creativity, it is most important that you hold onto your belief even through extreme disappointment. You must place your complete trust and faith in what you are doing. This Natural Law has a greater plan for your objective and if you remain faithful to your idea the Universe will deliver an opportunity so much better than the one previous. It is when you give up, you have failed. *Remember temporary defeat is not permanent failure.* There is an invincible power at work if you allow it to be.

THIRTEEN

Relationships

"You can search throughout the entire universe for someone who is more deserving of your love and affection than you are yourself, and that person is not to be found anywhere. You yourself, as much as anybody in the entire universe deserve your love and affection."
Buddha (c. 563-c. 483 BC)

When we first get into a wonderful relationship we see the person as special, we see them as almost flawless. We get caught up in this powerful energy when the exuberance of our emotions joins theirs. It is wonderful. It uplifts us. This feeling starts to change after a few months and we begin to see this person through different eyes. However, the person may not have changed, instead they might now be more comfortable to be themselves; they have just landed on the ground from the platform we've had them on for awhile. The problem is, with these relationships, many of us want to believe this person will fulfill all of our expectations, you know, the ones we have made conditional to our list. We believe this person we are searching for, this ideal being will make us happy. Consequently, when the relationship becomes more familiar, we begin to see that person's flaws and sometimes disappointment sets in. We feel that they have let us down.

A healthy relationship is one where flaws are accepted, where each one shows respect for the other person and understands that each person is distinct with their own individuality. Appreciation is a given, which builds a strong foundation for all the ups and downs the relationship will face, which are many. This kind of commitment brings with it a high energy frequency. But, before we can really have a completely committed relationship with anyone, we have to love ourselves first. We cannot expect another person to make us completely happy if we ourselves don't see our own worth. When we are not seeing ourselves as truly deserving of love, we repel it without even knowing. We hold on to a low energy frequency and give that out to others. This frequency will give a signal to others that you do not need love and compassion because that is the message which you are sending out before you.

Your work is to be kind and compassionate to yourself first. We have to really love ourselves. Do you see? You have to be a friend to yourself first and then you attract it back to you in kind and loving friends and relationships.

Many people repeat negative relationships, which are abusive physically or mentally. They do this because they feel they cannot move forward out of this box of unworthiness they have put themselves in. They feel inferior, unloved and even insignificant. All of which draws low energy fields that surround them. This sort of relationship is fragile at best. Anger is displayed often, which can only cripple any positive growth. People in these relationships have never considered their own merits in life or their value, believing they have none and deserve what is given to them. Everyone on this Earth has value. Everyone is worthy of being loved and giving love, albeit, no one can get by this self imposed box if they can't see the possibilities of their own worth.

The first gift to yourself to move through any negative relationship is to truly look into the way you think about yourself. You do this with love for yourself and with honesty. You have to reprogram your thoughts to believe you really don't need someone else to give value to you. This is the way you change those old messages. This is done with kindness and compassion. This is where positive affirmations enhance this process to move you from where you are.

If we cannot love ourselves, then we cannot give love with our full ability and we cannot receive it. If we think we are undeserving of a compassionate relationship then what we expect is what we are given. This repeats itself constantly. This happens through the Law of Attraction. What you give out in energy you draw back to you. If you don't see yourself as lovable, others you come into contact with won't see you as lovable either. Like attracts Like. It is a Universal Law. When you see yourself as lovable you feel it deep within, you then attract relationships that are in likeness of yourself, loveable, caring people.

There are many people that find suitable partners only to sabotage the relationship by criticizing them and placing their own unrealistic demands on that person without understanding that he or she cannot achieve what is wished for—it is unrealistic to expect that person to reach an impractical goal. If you are stuck in this way of thinking then you will feel the disapproval and reproach you give because this hurt can only come back to you. It has no other place to go. It cannot move forward when it is in an unhealthy place. It is as if you are shouting from the mountain top, *"Here I am shower me with all the hurtful ways and words possible,"* because what you have put out, you will receive in some way or form.

When you draw kindness and compassion towards yourself you also draw people of like.

Forgiveness

Some people have had to look to forgiveness in their life to move forward to a more healthy lifestyle. This means they have had to forgive the people that have hurt them in their past and let it go. When you finally let this energy go into the Universe it dissipates and you actually move from that low energy field to a much higher frequency. This is another way to move forward to a more healthier relationship.

Ask yourself these questions:

Is there a need for me to forgive someone?

Is there a need to forgive myself?

Can I forgive them, or myself?

What caused them to act that way, or say what they have said to me?

Although it may not seem logical to us, we have to try and understand why this person did what they did to us. It may be entirely distorted, we may not agree with them, but we have to forgive them and release it because this is the chain that holds us where we are. We cannot move on from this place until we do, or gain a healthy friendship or relationship.

Forgiveness is huge to move on from an old relationship or to build onto a relationship that already exists, if one of you has been injured through words or action. Sometimes it is a parent or a child we have to forgive, sometimes it is a spouse, partner, sibling or a friend. Whoever it is, if we cannot find it in ourselves to forgive them, we are the ones that suffer because we are the ones that live with the grief it causes. One thing is for sure, while you hold on to this distress you will never be completely happy with your life.

ccasionally you have to understand there are people that cannot face what they did to you. They are completely in denial not only with what they did to you, but within themselves, because perhaps what they have done to you is too hard for them to face, so they really do convince themselves that they did not do it. They believe this. In this case there is one of two choices you can make which is: either you accept this. You are aware that this is the only way they can handle what they have done to you and forgive them while allowing them to still be a part of your life, or forgive them and move on without them and let it go. Either choice will be beneficial to you because it gives to you the freedom of letting this low energy system dissolve.

Also we, ourselves, may live in denial of something we cannot face. We may have done or said something unacceptable and damaged a relationship. It is with remorse for what we have done that we may confront this situation, and as a result we have to attempt to give an apology to the person we have wronged before we can possibly move forward. They may never accept our apology but if this is the case and we clearly own what we have done and feel our remorse, we may then forgive ourselves and move on. This is the only way we can move forward from this condemnation that has come upon us. It is not expected from a loving Universe that we should live with this mistake for the remaining years of our lives. This will not help anyone for that matter. Forgiveness is acceptance and sometimes we bring more reproach on ourselves than we deserve.

This is where we really let go and move forward, we give up any hope of changing the past.

A healthy relationship is sharing and supporting each other through our decisions in life. It is the comfortable feeling when someone has your back, and they care for you even with all of your faults and in return you care for them. It is not a one way street. It is work in progress for both people for the entire time you are together. It is respect. It isn't always easy but if you think of this person in gratitude for all that he or she has brought to your relationship, you will see them constantly in a positive light. We oftentimes fall into the negative field and take each other for granted. This is where we walk through the entrance of the low energy field. This is where we start to stray into deep waters and lose our way in the relationship if we are not careful and aware. We all have moments of this which are healthy, however, it is when we fall into this constantly, starting to blame one another frequently, when we lose sight of any goodness the person holds. Sometimes we or our partner become so lost in these ways it becomes virtually impossible to retrieve the relationship. To get through this it is advisable you keep a list close by of all the good characteristics of this person. Read it often, remind yourself of their worth and thank them often. To be appreciative is the highest of honors you can bestow on anyone. We all love the people that cherish our values, and we all need to be valued. Remember when you learn to appreciate, you are activating reverence back to you.

however, those who have inflicted horrendous pain on another will be given this back in the way it was extended. It will show up in their lives at some point. This is the way this Natural Law works, it does not fail.

There is a warning to be nurtured in looking for a relationship. Keep in mind, we can ask and expect wonderful relationships, but we cannot expect to force a person who we have a fancy for, to suddenly fall head over heels in love with us if they don't have the will to do so. No person on this earth should try and gain control over another person. Using your thoughts will not bring this person to you no matter how you try, it just won't happen. We all have the freedom of thought and therefore the freedom to desire. We have complete control over our own lives but if we try to control anyone else, it will eventually backfire on us with more force than a legion of warriors ready for battle. This also is something to keep in mind of anything we ask for, it must be harmonious with this Universal Law. We cannot violate the rights of others. Our best well-being will be conserved by a conscious cooperation with the Great Whole, God or the Universe, they are the same.

Always give gratitude for all the relationships in your life, try to do this with passion and feeling. You will then see those wonderful relationships become even more awesome because gratitude expands life and love. It really does seal the deal.

I offer this affirmation as a helpful tool to bring all of those relationships back into your life that may have been drifting away from you.

"I love all the wonderful times I experience with my family and friends."

Repeat this often, make it your habit.

Remember you are an exclusive individual, your mind is dazzling with brilliance. You are not alone, you never were. You just have to claim what is yours and if a loving relationship is what you want, then be a loving person and it will come. You will attract it. Try it, what have you to lose?

Over to W.T...

FOURTEEN

What are you Chasing?

*"Whatever the mind of man can conceive
and believe, it can achieve."*
W. Clement Stone (1902-2002)

Money, money, money. It is why we get up in the morning. It is why we sit in traffic, fight the weather, go to work with a cold, rush through life, all for the pursuit of money. If only we had a lot of money, things would be so easy, or so we think. But is money all you need to be satisfied? Is this really the main thing you need?

I have always had enough money to live a middle class life, or at least close to middle class when I was in my twenties. Money brings security and stability into your life. We all want it and need it, to deny yourself of it is ridiculous, so when I asked myself the question—*what are you chasing?* I needed to dig deeper to see what was *really* driving me. I needed to understand money is the fruit that I will reap but the work that I do must make me happy. Life is supposed to be fun and wonderful. If the way I make my money leaves me miserable when I get home, is the money worth the lack of quality of life? I found what I am chasing isn really money, it is happiness. So I needed to make some rules I could follow; a guideline for my life, and a blueprint to ensure I was pursuing joy and happiness as defined by me.

Rule # 1. Do Things That Make Me Happy

Play music, watch a comedy, joke around, relax and have fun. Life is supposed to be exciting and wonderful. It starts in the morning with how you start your day. Each day I will try to be happy knowing I have another day to chase my goals. I will be thankful for what I have and grateful for my abilities to affect the outcome. I will strive to make those around me happy.

This is something I practice every day. It doesn't come natural, sometimes I forget to start out happy. I may be tired or not really excited about what the day will bring. Some days I have to find ways to make myself feel good or try to catch myself in a bad mood so I can correct it. Often my family will let me know or give me a hint. It helps.

Rule # 2. Smile

It is simple and easy to do. No one can take it away from you and it doesn't cost you anything. Always remember to smile.

...le # 3. Surround Yourself With Positive People

Keep the nay-sayers away from you. A positive environment will nurture your mind and belief in yourself. Never let someone stop you from your goals and dampen your attitude.

People don't like it when they see you happy all the time, if they're not happy.

They get jealous and feel like you have it so easy. Instead of asking you how you are able to stay positive all the time so they may be happy too, they would rather try to bring you down to their level of happiness. Don't get sucked in. Be strong and stay focused on your happiness. Remember you are the only one that gets to live your life.

Rule # 4. Be Grateful For The Little Things

Anytime you are doing something you like or something relaxing or something that is easy, be grateful. Make time to do things that make you feel good. Smile. Laugh, have fun.

Too often we are busy taking the kids to activities, helping with homework, working over-time, cooking, cleaning, running around. We forget to enjoy life. We should enjoy life for at least a few minutes every day. Stop and acknowledge when you are doing something that makes you feel good, don't take it for granted for you never know when you will be able to have that moment again.

Rule # 5. Don't Get Caught Up In The Drama

There will always be those around you who have some type of perceived crisis.

Focus on what you want in your life. Don't make their problems your problems. If you have drama in your life, try to find a positive side to it. There is always a positive side. Focus on that and feel good about it.

Rule # 6. See The Good Things Around You And In The World

There are a lot of good things for you to see. Don't let the news get you down. Don't focus on all the problems of society. Notice the old man and old lady walking down the street holding hands, the mother playing with her kids, the sunset, the fresh air, the sounds of life all around you.

This sounds corny but this is the thing, you can get wrapped up in all kinds of issues on the news and be afraid to do anything or go anywhere. All the while other people are living their lives and enjoying the world so why shouldn't you? Look for good things and you will start to notice them in your environment.

~ule # 7. Throw Doubt Out

Doubt and fear will stop you from doing the things you can accomplish. Everyone second guesses themselves but you have to ignore it and go for it.

Rules # 8, 9, & 10. Build Strong Relationships

Care about people, say thank you, take the time to stop and ask your friends how things are, listen, say I love you whenever, give people hugs, be honest, be kind and be happy. What good is success if you do not have people you care about to share it with? What good is success if you've had to hurt someone to get it? What good is success if you are not happy? I know this is cheesy but some of the best things for you, may sound like someone just took one too many happy pills. Like I said, you are the only one that can live your life so make it the best life you can.

Once I wrote my rules, the next step was to train my brain to focus on these rules and make them a part of my subconscious. Repetition is the tool I used. I would read the rules each night before I would go to bed. I did this for a few weeks, adding other notes to it. I kept this routine in some form or another and I still do this now. As you will read later, my notes kept getting larger until I realized I was writing some type of book. I was writing a book to myself. Weird!!!

We live in a world that is affected by our feelings. How w
feel will bring more of those feelings into our lives. What I
had to learn was how to read my feelings.

Sure I had rules and routines, but if I didn't make a conscious
effort to control my feelings all the cheesy and corny words
wouldn't help anything. I know how I feel when I am happy
and I know how I feel when I am not. I had to catch myself
when I was feeling badly and find a way to change my
mood. What I found out from the *Master Key System* is that
your thoughts control your feelings. Control what you are
thinking about, and you control your feelings.

This is called correct thinking. We have to read our feelings
and adjust our thinking to bring the feeling of joy, happiness,
and confidence into our life. The technique is to concentrate
on what we want to think about. The first thing I did is ask
myself,

What is on my mind most of the day?

Until I asked this question, my mind was all over the place.
It could change by the minute. I had to learn how to use the
power of concentration to control my thoughts and stay focused
on what I wanted to think about. I touched on this earlier but
it is good to repeat it as I am a firm believer in the power of
repetition. To focus our thinking we need to write down what
we want our future to look like. Details should not be spared.

Write about your health, your career, your relationships, your wealth, your happiness, your wants and desires.

Training our thoughts to become habitual will take time, practice and consistency. Don't let your focus sway to other things. This is where holding big ideas and big pursuits will be a key in helping you focus. Remember the rich do this and this brings great results. It is one of the secrets to success. You need to focus on the end result until it is achieved, believing it will happen, knowing your success is guaranteed.

Expect greatness; make no apologies for your ambitions, reach for you goal, achieve it and then set higher goals. Always keep reaching, never be satisfied, stay hungry and enjoy the road you travel.

Once I had my rules in place and I knew I was chasing Joy and Happiness, I realized these things are only valuable and profitable if you have great health so...

Rule # 11. Invest In Your Health.

Always take care of your health and be grateful for your health. Rejuvenate your body and invest in your well-being. Success without health cannot be enjoyed for long.

Too often you invest in your education, you invest in your mind and your understanding of the world around you. You

pursue success and financial security but you never stop t
think about your health. The body is like a machine, if it is
looked after properly it will last you a long time. I fell in love
with the gym many years ago and I made a pledge to myself,
as long as I am healthy and able I would always go to the
gym. I love the fact that anything you don't like with your
body you can change with a bit of hard work and routine.
You can go on the internet, learn how to target whatever
area you want to change, and you can track the results. The
best part of it all is, when you reach financial success you
will be able to enjoy it without restrictions or bottles full of
medications just because you invested in your health and
well-being now. Exercise is a great way to manage stress too.
Nothing can get rid of a stressful day like lifting something
heavy or going for a hard run. Leave it all at the gym, burn
it all off in the weight room, use the stress to drive you,
motivate you to push harder and dig deeper. When you
are done you feel cleansed and happy, most of the time you
even forget why you were stressed or it doesn't seem to be a
big deal anymore.

Make this a part of your goal for success. Be fit, be strong,
and be a champion of stress.

These are my rules for my success. I hope they inspire you
to write your rules for your success.

I am chasing joy and happiness; what are you chasing?

Back to Pamela...

FIFTEEN

Your Invincible Power

"When you are inspired by some great purpose, some extraordinary project, all your thoughts break their bonds; your mind transcends limitations, your consciousness expands in every direction, and you find yourself in a new, great and wonderful world. Dormant forces, faculties and talents become alive, and you discover yourself to be a greater person by far than you ever dreamed yourself to be."
Patanjali Yoga (c. 200 BC)-Sutras.

Through great works of dexterity we have seen wonders with architecture, mastery in literature and magnificent works of regal quality in the arts, which all represent high energy fields. Within these energy fields, through his or her thoughts, the artist found the highest spiritual order. Out of confusion came commitment and out of commitment came greatness. To give love through creativity is our greatest gift to ourselves. We capture the idea of what we would most want to do through our thoughts combined with our love and feelings for it.

Consider that each inventor there ever was or ever will be started to invent with a thought. The thought became larger and then extremely compelling, added was inspiration and energy, and then feeling. The feeling of wanting to complete this invention, a feeling of a quiet excitement, of reaching their absolute goal. The thought took on its own life and hence, electricity, your cell phone, computers, you being able to text people, in fact all of this technology we use today came from a thought, and every invention big or small, started the same way. Can you argue with this?

We believe all of the amazing programs technology gives to us because we see it before our eyes. Most of us don't understand how words can be texted across the world in seconds, but we know this happens. None of this could happen if the inventor couldn't connect with the deeper part of himself. Anyone who creates connects with forces beyond what we can recognize in our external world. These powerful forces are Divine Intervention from a loving Universe. Read the works of any famous inventor and he will confirm he wasn't alone in the process of his invention. Ask a writer, an artist anyone who is committed with love for what they are doing. They connect with invincible powers.

Astonishing inventions with technology is happening constantly that a hundred years ago, had we been born then, we would have laughed at, and we would have felt none of this could ever be possible—but it is. So why do we question that our thoughts don't have power when there is proof everyday?

hen we laugh at this concept, we let those who are familiar with this concept, have all the power. We then go through our life merely existing, scrambling for the scraps of life the well-informed souls around us throw our way. We don't see what life is telling us. We don't see our own worth. We only see lack and limitation.

To find our own thoughts of creativity is to open our eyes and heart to the things we really love. We all have talents that are bursting for us to discover them. We are creative humans. There are many different ways for our creativeness to show up in our lives. It has been doing so all along, you just weren't aware of it.

We need to look within ourselves and omit complaint, blame, and negativities. In this way we can move on to circumstances that are more positive which leads to happiness. This is how we gain power over our own life and make vast changes to it.

The Law of Attraction or The Law of Love, They Are Both The Same

This Natural Law has also been called the Law of Love, because we have to love ourselves first, if we cannot love ourselves we cannot give to others with harmony, and this in turn affects our creativity. This is why it is important to take the time for ourselves and care for ourselves first. However, this doesn't mean we should be selfish, it means to stop the abuse in our thought processes we have been accustomed to most of our lives. It means to be kind to ourselves and to trust that we can be powerful. It is our right to have all we want in life. You are here for a reason and the reason is to be Happy and Abundant with Love, Wealth and Health, which in turn brings to you all what you desire.

When we can become all we have wanted to be we can give all that we want to give back to this world. Remember, each of us that helps the other, not only uplifts ourselves but also uplifts our fellow man. This in turn lifts the energy of all on this Earth. So you see, there is a most valuable reason for each one of us to realize our invincible power!

A Lesson In Survival

Naturally when we hear of a change in our routine, whether at work or some situation out of *'what we call the ordinary,'* we allow our emotions to take place. We may not know how these changes may happen or even if they will happen, but the majority of us feel a panic deep within us when a change is presented. We give in to assumptions which are usually negative and our emotions then give in to panic.

Humankind has a past history of emotional survival which meant we had to maintain a skeptical uncertainty of life to survive. We had to be on guard and suspicious of our fellow ian. These instincts have been implanted in us. This is why we resist change. This is why we see most changes as a threat.

Freedom from this way of negative thinking is what life now presents to us in its place by virtue of this Natural Law. Once we accept this law, we have stepped away from our old survival instincts, we have moved towards new ideas. We open our eyes and see this Natural Law does not work in the limited way we have come to know as our, 'logic' since the thread of our logic is woven with negativity from our external world.

The thread of this Natural Law is powerful, solid and unfailing. If we follow this law by using positive, harmonious thoughts, we will see this law holds our best interest at heart and it will work in our lives in a way that we could not have dreamed of.

Fifteen percent of positive thinking counterbalances the eighty five percent of the worlds negative thinkers. So each one of us that can change our thoughts from mostly negative to positive can help to uplift our fellow man to a greater degree. A few loving thoughts counterbalances all of our negative thoughts. This is how powerful each of us are, and this is how we make a difference not only in our lives but in the world collectively.

We are all valuable people. We all deserve love. We all deserve to be happy. We all deserve to be rich. To receive this is to believe in your own ability to make the changes necessary.

Feelings

Think about the last time you were really motivated and excited about something or a situation in your life. How did you feel? When you know what you want in life, when your desire reveals itself, the feelings you put into it are the glue to make it work and stick to you. You have to feel that same excitement and motivation you felt the time previously. Your focus needs to be so deep nothing can stop you from pressing on with your plan to attract this desire into your life. You do this with your will. A great affirmation to assist with this is, '*I can be all I will to be.*' You have to repeat this often.

This affirmation carries with it a strong energy frequency. It is a strong positive statement. When you say it you must add feeling and mean it, make it stick to you. You'll be surprised how powerful this statement is and how it will push you forward.

People fail because they start to bring the, 'if' into their plans. The 'if' is a preview to doubt, 'If I do this that way maybe it will go wrong,' 'If people know about my idea they may laugh.' If carries doubt on its back. I get around this by constantly being aware that if and doubt are strongly attached to low energy fields. When a thought attaches to a low frequency it cannot move forward. It only lingers for awhile and eventually dissipates.

You see it only has one place to go and this is why so many people's ideas fail. Although their ideas had great possibilities, those ideas came and then left.

Replace the 'if' with 'When.' When carries a high frequency. It is loaded with energy. You can feel this as you attach it with your desire, 'When I get my desire.' 'When this plan materializes...' Can you hear the strength that comes with 'When' as you say it compared to 'If?'

This is why it is important to use strong words.

Make your desire large. Remember there is no limit to what you want to do or have. The necessary requirements for this is that your desire and plans must not be harmful to any living person or thing, inasmuch as everything on this planet and beyond is sustained with living energy. So make sure your desire is in harmony with this Natural Law.

This is Your Invincible Power. Believe in this power, it is yours if you claim it.

My story... I have been blessed to have had a loving mom and dad. My mom put me and my three sisters and a brother first. Our best interest was at her heart. She had a rough background, herself, and raised her own sisters and brothers and gave us all mountains of love. I was born and raised on a council estate in, Leicester, England. We were far removed from being well off. My mom and dad struggled from week to week, however, as children, we were rich in love, and our childhood was absolutely full of adventure and positive experiences.

My mom always saw the best in me and constantly built me up. What she couldn't give to me was education. In those days, girls weren't expected to work after they graduated at fifteen, which was the full requirement of secondary education at that time. They were expected to leave school, eventually get married and live off of their husbands wage, while they raised the children. It was the way of life at that time. Everyone was in the same boat so it wasn't anything us girls questioned. My brother was educated... well he was the only male out of the siblings, so he was expected to be the breadwinner of his family when he eventually had one.

Life in the late 60's changed drastically. We women did go to work and most of us kept on working. I have always worked and have been fortunate to have had fairly well paid jobs. I became a supervisor in a job that called for three years of college. I still didn't have any more education than what I had graduated with. I then got another job working along with Child and Youth Workers, doing the same job as they did, even training new C.Y.W's on the job. This required three years of college, or more. I have somehow been able to slip into these positions through the back door of life, so to speak. I believe now it was because I just thought I could. My mom gave me the idea that I could do anything and so I ran with it... I guess. I never thought about the ifs I just did it. I have never had a need to delve into the why's of it until this last year and a half, when this natural law was presented to me. I just knew that if you put your mind to anything, that you could do it.

The Brain Gene

I don't want to put education down in any way because education is on a high energy frequency, providing it is used for the right reason. I just didn't have a choice, and then I didn't feel the need for it. Many people I have worked with in jobs other people have put down to being menial, have been amazingly sharp with ingenious logical reasoning. I have learned considerably from their wise intelligence. I have learned never to look down on people in any job, as you do not know their story and the reason why they are there. I know that each and every one of us have the brain gene and we all can be brilliant, we just haven't come to this realization yet. When we do, life will become a completely different place. We will all create intelligently and our lives will feel worthy.

My Failure...

I did however have a love for writing from when I first went to school. I have a diploma for creative writing. I had written two novels, but this is also where I failed myself. I was immensely focused on the first novel I wrote. It is an historical, murder mystery. I loved every minute of the journey of writing it. After the manuscript was finished, I started to send it to publishers. I did this with complete doubt in my mind and questioned myself constantly. I always ran on low energy vibes. I couldn't bring myself to step out of it and of course I got rejection slip after rejection slip. The second fiction novel has never gone to a publisher.

In spite of this fact, I had been fairly successful in my other prior endeavors, however, my confidence didn't span out to that sphere of my creative field. This is where my self-assurance lacked. I was living constantly, at that time, with the undercurrent messages which are attached to fear. The doubts stacked up against me and I believed them. I gave up.

However;, I always had my mom's voice in the background telling me how valuable I am. I often asked myself, why was I so fortunate to have had such a wonderful mom, dad and family, and then to marry a loving husband who is kind and considerate and also believes in me, and have three wonderful sons, and their families, and the list goes on. I then watched the movie *'The Secret,'* and I read the book.

The more I was taking this knowledge in of this Natural Law, the more I realized every pathway we take, every incident that presents itself and every choice we make brings with it a powerful meaning. I had to sit and contemplate why this and that happened to me. With those thoughts, again the question posed itself to me, has it had many times prior, which was, *'Why did I end up working for the Children's Aide Society?'*

I had struggled with this job at times due to my not being educated professionally. I had stumbled through it, learning from my fellow workers each day. In essence, I did this job the only way I knew how to, through my heart, as I put myself in the people's shoes who were involved. It was hard at times but rewarding and my eyes became open to the conflict and the uncertainty these people live with daily. I had to ask myself constantly: *'Would I have made those choices had I been born without guidance and love?'* There was never an answer, how could there be?

You see, those of us that have been fortunate to have had parental guidance, love, and a decent quality of upbringing, do not really understand the struggles of those that face a daily lifestyle of adversities mostly starting from their birth. Do we have the right to judge them? Most definitely not.

"Being unwanted, unloved, uncared for, forgotten by everybody, I think that is a much greater hunger, a much greater poverty than the person who has nothing to eat." Mother Teresa (1910-1997)

With this view in mind I came to understand my journey in life-it has taken me awhile, but I arrived! I knew instantly what I was here for and why I was so fortunate. I have to give back. I was to help spread the word.

When this idea presented itself through a sequence of events, that I should write this book, my first thoughts were, there was so many books on the Law of Attraction, I have read so many myself. And then the answer came with strong energy vibrations, the more we work together to talk about this Invincible Natural Law the more positive energy we inject and the impact eventually will be tremendous. When W.T presented his work to me I hadn't a clue he had been writing. Although his way of putting things is very different from my own, I believe it works.

The message I hope to convey to you through these words are: Wherever you are, under whatever circumstances you were born into, you have been given the freedom of choice. This is not false hope, I would never do that. It is an infallible, invincible law. It doesn't matter who failed you in this external world because once you have joined forces with this Powerful Natural Law, you will see the greatest changes in your life that you could ever hope to see and all you have to do is believe. I am on the wonderful path of adding to the positive energy field to help lift everyone else. How about you? I hope that you will join me and W.T on this journey!

So you see, you are my main focus, each and every one of you, just as I was my mom's.

This is my loving gift to you, I hope you can accept it with all of the love and feelings I have put into it for you.

Our desire is that you can see the sincerity of a loving Universe that will always place you first. Just Believe, and it will bring you to Your Invincible Power.

Remember: You can be all you will to be!

From Your Loving Friends,

Pamela Hamilton and W. T. Hamilton.

"We must always remember that even with this knowledge, everything doesn't come to us wrapped up and tied in red ribbons. Life doesn't work like that. The Universe sends many tests to us along the way. It is how we view those tests and what we do with them that really counts." Pamela Hamilton.

SUMMARY

How to Understand and Apply What You Have Learned to Your Life

Throughout this book you have been given theoretical and practical applications. Within each chapter there have been lessons. Some chapters have exercises at the end, while other chapters are the exercise.

This book has been designed to be understood and applied in stages. It is important to understand each stage thoroughly in theory and application, before moving on to the next stage. This is why some exercises will take many days while others can be done as you grow your abilities to manifest.

This is not a book to read once, feel inspired and move on. You cannot know how to successfully use this knowledge just by quickly reading it. It is like going to the gym and learning how to do squats with weights. Just because you know how, doesn't mean you can start squatting 200lbs.

So first, read the chapter and do the exercise at the end of the chapter for the duration of days recommended. You don't need to rush through it now, you have already read the whole book. Now take the opportunity to invest the necessary time into your development, to really learn how to use this knowledge and apply it to your life.

Next, you will notice throughout this book we give you 'My Stories' You will also notice the majority of these stories take place before we learned the law of attraction. We purposely included these stories to highlight the fact, the Law of Attraction is always working in your life and has always been, whether you accept it or not. Take time to think about your own story and you will discover how your focus and attention on any given thing has shaped your life so far. You now have the power, Your Invincible Power, and can use the theory and practical application to write your new story, the life that you deserve.

Lastly, know that you are worth it. You are valuable and can be anything you tell yourself, without a doubt, you can be. It is time to use this book to build your inner strength. Empower yourself and shine.

Let's Look At Some Key Highlights And Things To Be Aware Of

1) Visualization is the tool for loading the subconscious.

There are many exercises and references to visualization in this book. Use them and make it part of your daily routine.

2) You cannot believe, until you change what you believe.

Throughout this book we have given you techniques to allow you to change the truths you tell yourself. We have included affirmations for you to use, Follow the instructions and add them to your daily routine.

3) Your relationship with yourself is the most important relationship you will ever have.

This is a key part of empowerment. It is the beginning of having. Be conscious of how you value yourself. We have given you examples in this book of the little things we tell ourselves that turn out to be self-sabotaging. Make note of these examples and remove them from both your vocabulary and your thinking. As part of your daily routine mentally tell yourself *"When I have,"* or, *"when I do."*

4) Everything takes time and time brings everything.

This is a journey. Give yourself time to understand not only the concepts and theories in this book but also how to apply it to your life and situation. Give each chapter time to resonate before you move on to the next one. As you work through the book, make notes of the key points in each chapter and review them monthly over the course of 12 months.

5) Your daily routine should always include this; Gratitude.

You need to make a daily routine now, that includes gratitude in various ways. Your daily routine should include:

A) 2-3 affirmations to be recited each morning, followed by 5 things to be grateful for, and a moment in the morning for Your Time.

B) During the day, monitor your self talk, take a moment to visit the picture of your future experience.

C) Each night practice the exercise in the chapter you're on.

D) Make sure throughout this book and beyond you take time to sit and visualize each day. This will now be a part of your daily routine to bring all the wonderful things you desire and want into your life.

E) Make daily entries into your Gratitude Journal. Do not take a break from this routine. Maintain a gratitude journal as well as a goals journal and keep them growing. Make entries into the gratitude journal daily.

AFFIRMATIONS

Here are some affirmations you can use daily. Pick two or three that connect with you and say them as frequently as possible throughout your day. The idea behind this is to reprogram your subconscious mind; your subconscious needs to be fed repetition to bring you to the life of your desire.

Value

I can be all I will to be.
I am valued and loved.
I am a valuable person and deserve love and respect to flow into my life.
I am grateful for each positive experience in my life.
I love all the wonderful times I experience with my family and friends.
Life loves me and protects me.
Life loves me, and all my needs are blessed with this love at all times.
I am greeted with smiles and love wherever I go today.
I love life, and life loves me.
Everything in my life is working out for my higher good.

Forgiveness

With love I release this incident in my life and let it go.
I set myself free from this situation and allow positive energy to re-enter my life.
I love and forgive myself.

Wealth

I am worthy of abundance.
I am completely grateful for all of the money that comes my way.
I appreciate and feel blessed with all of the abundance that flows into my life.
I gratefully accept all the extra income that comes my way.
My income is constantly increasing.

Health

I am thankful that my body will heal itself.
I am grateful that every part of me is healthy.
I prosper wherever I go in health, wealth and joy.
I trust my powerful brain cells to give me an abundance of health.
Thank you, all you powerful brain cells that are keeping me healthy.

I am whole, perfect, strong, powerful, harmonious, loving and happy.
I embrace the pure Energy that flows within me, it is always ideal and healthy.

Remember, if your thoughts are in harmony with the creative Principles of this Natural Law, it is in tune with the Infinite Mind, and it will form the circuit, which means your desire will manifest, it will not return to you void. Just believe.

Congratulations! You have completed the first reading of this book. We are very proud of you and also very impressed. As a reward for your dedication into your personal development we want to give you a bonus gift.

Here is a key way to enhance your visualization.

Find a quiet place where you can sit in silence for 10-15 minutes. Sit in an upright position. Close your eyes and breathe in slowly and deeply through your nose, filling your lungs and contracting your belly, holding your breath for a second and then slowly releasing it through your mouth. Focus on your breathing rhythm for 10 to 12 breaths. Now either out loud or in your mind, while breathing out, repeat the words, *'I Can Be All I Will to Be.'* Repeat it 17 times while keeping the same breathing pattern. Do this each time you start your visualization session. Once you have completed this part, then go to the next part of the visualization, which is focusing on the experience you want to have. Seeing in detail what you want to experience until it becomes like a memory of an experience you've already had.

This is your gift for completing this book in it's entirety. Use this as you read the book again and practice the exercises in each chapter.

See it in your mind over and over again until you see it in your presence-W.T. Hamilton

ACKNOWLEDGEMENTS

From Pam,

With endless gratitude I thank my dear husband, Clinton for constantly reminding me not to give up with my writing. To my son W.T with great thanks for coming on board and opening up his private life to enlighten others on their journey by making it fun and inspiring. I so appreciate my sons Scott and Warren for being there with an open heart and mind to listen to all of my ideas. Becky Thompson for reminding me of my pathway when at times I felt a little dismayed. Fanny Newport for her unbounded support. I thank my amazing grandchildren who keep me in laughter and show so much love, Clinton jr, Brehanna, Khai-Leigh, M.Jay, Ema-Leigh and Tiffany.

I give immense acknowledgment and gratitude to Sherry Brantley for all of her hard work and patients editing this book.

And supreme appreciation for all of those teachers that came before us to light the way.

I give boundless gratitude to my Source, God, my Inner Being for opening the door of this wonderful journey I am now on.

I give complete gratitude and love to all of you that are now taking this wonderful journey with me and my family, may you come into your own possession of Your Invincible Power.

From W.T.

Much love and gratitude to my family, who enrich my life with warmth, happiness and Tom Foolery. Much love to those who I see frequently and those who are there when it matters most.

A world of gratitude to my mentors Jim Britt and Jim Lutes for guiding me, encouraging growth and providing the change book platform to work with other like-minded souls.

Big ups to Kelli Locatelli, my social media mentor, for showing me the ways of the Purple Cow. Big ups to Misha Almira for teaching me how to market books. Big ups to Sherry Brantley for all her wonderful work editing our book.

Shout out to my awesome Conscious Change Expert team, (Patricia Rundblade, Sally Kay Miller, Kathryn Wilking, Michelle Gesky, Sherry Brantley) for following me on an idea and seeing it through to manifestation.

To the entire Change book community for all your support and love.

Big thank you's to Fanny Newport for your love and support, to my kids Clinton, Brehanna, MJay and Tiffany for keeping me young and always making me laugh.

And to my Mom (Pamela) and my Dad (Clinton) for giving me the confidence and swagger to believe in myself and do what I believe I can do.

ABOUT THE AUTHOR

Born in Leicester England, Pamela Hamilton has been writing since 1990. She has a diploma for Creative Writing with Highest Honors with the Stratford Career Institute of Toronto.

Along with her son W.T. Hamilton, she has written five nonfiction, inspirational books.

Pamela was first introduced to Universal Laws in the 1980's and became infatuated with them. Although she explored these laws for quite some time, it wasn't until 2012 that she pursued her studies diligently in these infinite Laws to find out how they work in one's life.

Pamela is a former worker of 'The Children's Aid Society of Oxford County.'

Pamela, along with W.T., have written a chapter in the tenth edition of *'The Change'* with nineteen other authors, along with Jim Lutes and Jim Britt.

Pamela now resides in Ontario, Canada.

Pamela is a Law of Attraction Expert and Vice President of *'Your Invincible Power'* Company which assists in going beyond suffering and finding the ultimate joy we all have a right to.

Born in Leicester England, W.T. Hamilton began writing in 2012. He used writing to figure out and understand these strange new theories his Mom had awoken him to. The content was originally intended to document, and prove or disprove the validity of Law of Attraction as he applied it to his life.

It was by the Law of Attraction that his work would become part of this book. Since writing this book, W.T. has become a mentor and coach. He is helping people discover their hidden potential by showing them how to turn their ideas into feasible products and services.

W.T. now resides in Ontario, Canada.

W.T. Hamilton is a Law of Attraction Expert and the President of '*Your Invincible Power*' Company.

You can find Pamela and W.T at www.wherethewindblows.ca

www.yourinvinciblepower.com

https://facebook.com/yourinvinciblepower

https://twitter.com/w_t_hamilton

http://twitter.com/yourfriendpam

success@yourinvinciblepower.com

http://www.selfgrowth.com/experts/wt-pamela-hamilton

Pamela is also an author on http://www.goodreads.com

Printed in the United States
By Bookmasters